C000213285

WALKS AROUND THE
ANCIENT CHURCHES OF LLŶN

Walks around
the Ancient Churches
of Llŷn

Christopher Nicholls

First published in 2013

© Text: Christopher Nicholls

ISBN: 978-1-84524-200-8
Cover design: Lynwen Jones

Published by Llygad Gwalch,
Ysgubor Plas, Llwyndyrys, Pwllheli, Gwynedd, Wales, LL53 6NG.
Tel: 01758 750432
e-mail: books@carreg-gwalch.com
www.carreg-gwalch.com

For Judith

Contents

Introduction

'All Llŷn is as it were a point into the sea'
John Leland, Itinerary in Wales, *circa* 1538

Ordnance Survey depicts a Llŷn that Leland would not have recognised. Whilst it would be unsurprising to learn that boundaries had been re-drawn since Leland's travels at the very dawn of the Reformation, it would surprise many to discover that for the native people of Llŷn – now in the twenty-first century – there has been no such re-defining of borders. Leland's 'point into the sea' describes perfectly the Llŷn they know: that narrow strip of land whose eastern border runs just west of the Eifl mountains in the north to the estuary of the Erch in Pwllheli harbour in the south. Those extended boundaries described by Ordnance Survey simply do not feature in local experience.

R. Gerallt Jones begins his charming and evocative memoir of a pre-war Llŷn boyhood, *A Place in the Mind*, like this:

> For me, born and bred within its boundaries, Llŷn was always a very clearly-defined locality. It had firm, rational frontiers, which made it, in effect, not a peninsula but an island, a circumscribed world of its own. On the southern side, Llŷn stopped at Pwllheli, for Pwllheli was the railhead and it was from Pwllheli that the railway train eventually took me away to school, to the hostile world where Welsh was no longer an acceptable linguistic currency. On the northern side, Llŷn came to an end when the road leading from Nefyn to Caernarfon climbed over the shoulder of Yr Eifl and descended to the alien village of Llanaelhaearn and the country beyond. Subjective though such a definition might be, it is the one I shall adopt, for it enclosed my childhood environment.

There is half a millennium separating Leland and Gerallt Jones, but if we were to go back a further 400 years, to the mid twelfth century, and consult, say, the stonemasons building St Hywyn's church in Aberdaron, they too would describe a Llŷn instantly familiar to their twenty-first century counterparts working on the sea-wall or tilling the fields of Uwchmynydd high above the village.

To unravel the mystery of Llŷn's borders we must look to the medieval map of the historic Kingdom of Gwynedd. Like all of the ancient Welsh kingdoms, Gwynedd was divided into a number of *cantrefi*. The *cantref* was the Welsh equivalent of the English 'hundred', a major administrative district. The area now defined by Ordnance Survey as 'The Llŷn Peninsula' comprises the old *cantref* (and, earlier still, kingdom) of Llŷn together with parts of the two neighbouring *cantrefi* of Arfon, to the north and west, and Eifionydd, to the south and east. Interestingly, the twenty-first century Diocesan map divides the Llŷn Peninsula into two Rural Deaneries: *Arfon*, which falls within the Archdeaconry of Bangor, and *Llŷn and Eifionydd*, which falls within the Archdeaconry of Meirionydd. Because they reflect the realities of life on Llŷn today and resonate so strongly with the medieval world of pilgrimage, you may find it interesting to be aware of these historic boundaries as you do the walks, three of which are in *Eifionydd* (Walks 1–3), eight in *Llŷn* (Walks 4–6 and 9–13), and two in *Arfon* (Walks 7 and 8).

It is worth noting that each of these districts has its own, distinctive topographical character: the wooded hinterlands of Eifionydd, the uncompromising mountain regions of Arfon, and the rural plains, volcanic hills and coasts of Llŷn. Pen Llŷn – literally, 'the head of Llŷn' – is the peninsula's westernmost tip, the area around Mynydd Rhiw, Aberdaron and Uwchmynydd. Bardsey Island (*Ynys Enlli*), the destination of pilgrims throughout the Middle Ages, lies a couple of miles off Pen Llŷn across the often violent waters of Bardsey Sound.

For me, John Leland's 'point into the sea' perfectly evokes

this finger of land not quite encircled by the sea. Not encircled but dominated nonetheless. There are few places in Llŷn where you are not aware either of the bright and glittering waters of Caernarfon Bay (*Bae Caernarfon*) to the north, or of the hazier, somehow more forgiving seas of Cardigan Bay (*Bae Ceredigion*) to the south. And from many places along the volcanic range of hills that form Llŷn's backbone you can see Cardigan Bay and Caernarfon Bay at the same time – on a clear day, with the Wicklow Mountains visible to the west and St David's Head hazy in the distant south. But if the north, south and western limits are bounded by the sea, to the east it is the mountains of Snowdonia (*Eryri*) that frame the horizon and dominate the imagination.

We have seen that the most ancient realities permeate and shape the everyday here in Llŷn even though, as Gerallt Jones wistfully acknowledges, everything changes, and not always for the better. In the case of Llŷn, however, such changes have been relatively gentle. Despite the best efforts of entrepreneurs such as the Victorian magnate Solomon Andrews, and in the 1930s, Billy Butlin, the peninsula remains largely unspoilt. It is perfectly possible, even in the height of summer, to walk its coastline or hills or rural lanes without seeing another soul, even though the peninsula is a mere thirty miles long and never more than twelve miles across. It is not at all far-fetched to assume that in the High Middle Ages the roads and sea-lanes of the peninsula were busier with pilgrims than they are now with tourists. Their final stopping off point on the mainland was Aberdaron at the peninsula's westernmost edge, in Leland's words, 'the very point into the sea'. Leland was more than likely making his brief and punchy notes on Llŷn in 1538. Leland says of the Aberdaron area that it is 'where there was of late a great pilgrimage'. What this innocuous-sounding note actually means is that in 1537 – the previous year – the abbey on Bardsey was 'dissolved' and its buildings destroyed, bringing 500 years of tumultuous tradition to a sudden end, like a mighty tree felled in a matter of minutes.

During the 1970s – some 450 years after Leland – the celebrated poet and priest R. S. Thomas was vicar of Aberdaron. He famously captured something of the particular quality of Llŷn, the smallest and, in my view, the loveliest of the western British peninsulas. His poem 'Retirement' begins:

> I have crawled out at last
> far as I dare on to a bough
> of country that is suspended
> between sky and sea

This slender bough of country between Caernarfon Bay and Cardigan Bay seems suspended not only in space but in time. There is an enchantment about Llŷn. It is a place of mysterious power and beauty where the earthly and the unearthly are intertwined and not always easy to distinguish.

The ancient churches of Llŷn
St Hywyn's, where Thomas spent the last eleven years of his ministry, perches at the very edge of the sea. Others of Llŷn's ancient churches crouch at the foot of mountains or shelter in wooded river-runs. They are Llŷn's hidden treasure. Walking to them is the perfect way to explore the varied and seductive charms of the peninsula. And there can surely be no better way to appreciate the churches themselves than by approaching them on foot, like those great processions of pilgrims during the Middle Ages but, equally, like those farmers and fishermen – the men, women and children of Llŷn – who, for a millennium and a half, made their often arduous way from remote and scattered homesteads on Sundays, High Days and Holy Days, and to mark the great rituals of birth, marriage and death.

The churches you will see on these walks are all medieval, typically built and improved between the twelfth and sixteenth centuries. Though the medieval presence of these churches is immediately apparent, their far more remote and ancient origins

11

are powerfully present too. All of the churches featured in these walks were founded in the fifth, sixth or seventh centuries. Whilst the simple wooden buildings of their founders have long since vanished, the stone medieval buildings sit within the ancient *llannau* – the sacred enclosures – founded by those wandering holy men at the dawn of Welsh Christianity. In Wales this very ancient presence has not been obliterated in the way that is typically the case elsewhere in Britain. There are two principal reasons for this: the locations of the *llannau* and the names of the *llannau*. Throughout Western Europe the majority of churches and monasteries are dedicated to supra-national saints, the great figures of the western tradition: John the Baptist, Saint Peter, Mary the Virgin and so on. In Wales, almost all of the dedications are to local figures, on the whole unknown outside Wales and the Celtic rim, some of whose identities are now lost to history even within Wales itself. But the presence of those early missionaries and solitaries is palpable, literally written into the landscape as the original *llan* and its founder comes to mean the village or town that eventually grew up around these holy places. Llangybi, for example, a small and pretty village in Eifionydd, means 'the *llan* of St Cybi' (Walk 3); Llanfaglan in Arfon, 'the *llan* of St Baglan' (Walk 7); and, in Llŷn, Llangwnnadl is 'the *llan* of St Gwynhoedl' (Walk 12).

But it is the 'wild, remote, uncompromising' *locations* of the churches that are even more powerfully evocative of the presence and preoccupations of the early saints than the names that they bear, as T. J. Hughes puts it:

Unlike elsewhere, the people did not build their churches at the places where they lived, chosen for safety or comfort or farmable land. Frequently instead, they built them at places chosen for reclusive prayer or for their sacred power, often wild, remote, uncompromising. And then, over time, they came to live there. It is an upturning of the order of things – a pattern of settlement in reverse, where the sacred has a generative role.

Who, then, were these 'saints' who built their *llannau* on the peninsula and on the mysterious island two miles off Pen Llŷn across the turbulent and treacherous waters of Bardsey Sound?

The Age of the Saints

Enid Roberts identifies the 200 years from around 450 to 650 as 'the golden age of the saints, the period when many of the *llannau* were established'. T. J. Hughes talks of the 'several hundred holy settlements' established during the mid to late sixth century, 'the *llans* of Wales and Herefordshire, the *lans* of Cornwall and Brittany'. These two centuries amount to a momentous and defining period in Welsh history, an epoch during which the physical, cultural and linguistic contours of what we now know as Wales emerged from the uncertain and dangerous world left behind by the Romans after their withdrawal from Britain at the beginning of the fifth century.

The Romans seem to have taken a pragmatic approach to the culture of the peoples they conquered, tolerating local custom and, wherever possible, adopting indigenous practices and beliefs into the dominant culture. There is evidence of a highly developed and integrated Romano-British culture in all the parts of the British Isles where the Roman Empire was entrenched. Three Romano-British bishops attended the First Council of Arles in 314, for example, one of them – Adelphius – possibly from Caerleon, the most important Roman garrison town in Wales. But the various invaders that swarmed into these islands in the wake of the Roman departure preferred to wipe out all trace of indigenous culture. And it was before these pagan, mainly Germanic invaders that native Britons fled from the Saxon-dominated lowlands of the south and east to the mountains and coasts of the north and west. These Celtic tribes were known to themselves as the 'Brythoniaid', from which the name 'Britain' derives.

Gildas, himself an early fifth-century Welsh saint, wrote *On the Ruin and Conquest of Britain*, one of the only two extant literary sources of evidence for life in Britain during this period. Referring to the laying waste of Britain he describes, in the language of an Old Testament prophet, the devastation wrought by the 'impious' Saxon hordes:

For the fire of righteous vengeance ... blazed from sea to sea, heaped up by the eastern band of impious men ... until it burnt nearly the whole surface of the land, and licked the western ocean with its red and savage tongue.

The migration of defeated Britons to the west and north he describes like this:

Some of the wretched remnant were consequently captured on the mountains and killed in heaps. Others, overcome by hunger, came and yielded themselves to the enemies, to be their slaves for ever ... others repaired to parts beyond the sea ... others, trusting their lives, always with apprehension of mind, to high hills, overhanging, precipitous, and fortified, and to dense forests and rocks of the sea, remained in their native land, though with fear.

The leaders of men amongst these scattered people were not only the princes but the saints too: sailing in their flimsy craft to Ireland and Gaul and other 'parts beyond the sea'; inhabiting the hostile, 'precipitous and fortified' mountainous regions of north Wales; peopling those 'rocks of the sea' like Bardsey and the islands near Llanbedrog settled by Tudwal and his followers.

It was during 'The Age of the Saints' that these dispersed Celtic peoples – the British diaspora, if you will – came to define their collective identity, an identity, as the historian John Davies puts it, 'chiefly based on a common religion and a common language'. This was the period when Welsh itself was forged, emerging as a distinct dialect of the ancient British tongue and a language in its own right. And it was when Christianity – a relatively minor cult even after the emperor Theodosius made it the official religion of the Roman Empire at the end of the fourth century – became the engine of the quest for nationhood. The founding myths of Wales are intimately bound up with the Celtic Church and its founding fathers.

The year 598 AD is commonly cited as the defining moment when Christianity began to take hold in Britain. This was the year when Augustine was sent by Pope Gregory to convert the heathen kingdom of Kent. But the history of Christianity in Wales began some 150 years prior to Augustine's historic mission. As we have seen, Christianity in Wales and the other Celtic heartlands was already putting down deep and vigorous roots by the middle of the fifth century. There were certain differences in custom between the Celtic Church and the Roman orthodoxy that Augustine had been despatched to promote. Five years after successfully establishing a Christian court in Kent, Augustine turned his attention to the anomalies he found in the Celtic Church. He convened a council in 602 at which he assumed the Welsh bishops would bow to his authority and fall in line with the orthodoxy on such controversial matters as the method for setting the date of Easter and the style of priestly tonsure. He was to be disappointed. His appeals or, rather, orders fell on deaf ears. His second attempt, in 604, was similarly stonewalled by the unrepentant leaders of the Welsh church. Of all the Celtic churches, the Welsh church was the last to conform to the orthodox Roman position and, even then, not until the Synod of Whitby sixty years later.

Amongst the earliest of the recorded Welsh saints was Madrun, the granddaughter of King Gwrtheyrn (Vortigern in English) whose last stand she witnessed before fleeing to the fort at nearby Garn Fadrun as Gwrtheyrn's camp on Tre'r Ceiri blazed and, as tradition has it, he was pursued to his death in the beautiful valley of Nant Gwrtheyrn below (Walk 8). Madrun is thought to have been born about 440. The story of Madrun and the fate of her father is a heady mix of history, myth and legend, its magical character illuminating underlying realities about the birth struggles of Wales and the early presence of Christianity, rather than providing a conventional historical narrative. The stories of other key early figures are more historically reliable, even if embellished, not unlike the fantastical decoration that illuminates the chronicles and holy books of later generations of saints and scholars.

Born perhaps a generation after Madrun, in the third quarter of the fifth century, St Illtud is of signal importance. Illtud, the son of a Breton prince, founded the famous monastery of Llanilltud Fawr in south-east Wales. This monastery and college was soon to become the crucible of Celtic Christianity. Its vast number of monks and scholars – reputedly around 2000 at its peak – were dedicated to the twin principles of learning and devotion and counted amongst their number almost all the major figures in the development of the early Celtic Church, including St David, St Patrick, St Gildas, and St Deiniol, the founder of Bangor cathedral and its first bishop. Illtud founded the monastery with the support of his great friend and mentor, St Dyfrig, probably the first of the great Welsh saints. At the time of the Synod of Llandewi Brefi, in 545, Dyfrig was the Archbishop of South Wales. He and Deiniol had persuaded the much younger Dewi – St David – to speak at the synod and, it is said, were so impressed by Dewi's eloquence that Dyfrig resigned his archiepiscopate in Dewi's favour. Dewi moved his See to St David's, and Dyfrig retired to Bardsey where he died not long after.

Modern scholarship tends to play down the idea that the 'Celtic Church' was an entity somehow separate from the mainstream of western Christianity, asserting that its differences were no more extreme or significant than the variations found in any regional church finding its way within the broad umbrella of emergent western Christendom. I think we can safely claim, however, that the early Celtic Church represented a very particular strand within Christendom. Whilst it prized the ascetic, solitary life, its effect was to strengthen community, and was instrumental in creating a kind of Celtic nationhood that transcended national borders, even as it crucially helped shape the emergent nation of Wales.

The 'saints' that roamed Wales in the fifth, sixth and seventh centuries – founding their *llannau*, acquiring followers even as they sought solitude, working wonders, establishing monasteries, leading missions, fostering learning and scholarship – were all of this Celtic nation: from Wales and Cornwall and Brittany and Ireland and *hen ogledd*, or the Old North. The Old North, the region roughly equivalent to modern southern Scotland and northern England, was a stronghold of British culture and language and the birthplace of many of the early saints. Elmet, an area of the Old North somewhere near where Leeds is today, was the birthplace of one Aliortus, a British Christian whose spectacular late fifth century memorial stone is to be found inside the church at Llanaelhearn (Walk 8). Gildas, whose account of the 'ruin of Britain' is quoted above, was also a native of the Old North, although revered as a Welsh saint. His compatriot, Deiniol, son of King Dunaut of the northern Pennines, became a major figure in the history of the Welsh church, having founded the cathedral in Bangor that still bears his name. Deiniol is amongst the many early church fathers buried on Bardsey. Cadfan, who founded the monastery on Bardsey, and his companions – Maelrhys (Walk 6) and Hywyn (Walk 13) among them – were all Bretons who had studied under St Illtud at the great monastery at Llanilltudd Fawr. This wider Celtic world was connected by language and by religion but was connected also in a more direct and physical way. In her enlightening book, *Bardsey Bound*, Enid Roberts discusses this connection:

> In the early ages, the sea provided much traversed, popular travel routes; it was easier and safer to journey by sea than to

face the dangers of vast forests and swamps on land. Archaeologists speak of the western sea-routes from the Mediterranean, with the north African coastline on one side and that of south Europe on the other, passing between the pillars of Hercules (the Straits of Gibraltar), reaching the western peninsulas – Brittany, Cornwall, Pembroke, Llŷn, Anglesey and Ireland. The sea was a means of joining these places together, not of separating them from one another.

It is likely that these trade routes were active as early as the late Stone Age, recent archaeological finds have unearthed material from Mynydd Rhiw's stone-axe 'factory' in surprisingly far-flung places. This picture of long-established trade and cultural routes between Wales and the Mediterranean is a convincing and inspiring one, surely giving the lie to any idea of the Celtic Church as an insular organisation cut off from the great cultural and intellectual currents of mainstream Europe – currents that included, for example, the monastic movement of the Desert Fathers of Egypt and Syria. Possibly the Celtic Church's defining characteristic was its focus on the monastery as the central feature of church organisation rather than the diocese, on the status of the abbot rather than the bishop. It is surely the case that the cultural exchange consequent upon the Mediterranean trade routes had a significant influence on this defining feature of early Welsh Christianity. Even after the Synod of Whitby when the Welsh church fell in line with the contested orthodoxies that had so exercised Augustine, the Celtic Church, not least in Wales, continued to develop along monastic lines. These monasteries, the *clasau*, were very different entities to the monasteries that grew exponentially after the Norman Conquest, the monasteries with which we are all familiar. Enid Roberts says this of the *clas*:

Briefly, a *clas* was a church with a community of men, women and families living a religious life under a leader or superior: Welsh priests never accepted celibacy. Several of the clas would be priests, ministering not only to nearby communities but also travelling further afield, establishing new churches, returning from time to time to their teacher, their father in God at the clas: thus the original little church became the mother-church of a large area.

In Llŷn, there were two *clasau*, one at Aberdaron, the other at Clynnog Fawr. Clynnog Fawr was founded by St Beuno sometime in the early seventh century. Beuno, the son of a prince of Powys, was of a later generation than the first great wave of saints to settle in Llŷn but he was to become, you might say, the patron saint of north-west Wales, the saint to whom there are more churches dedicated in this region than any other, eight if the disputed dedication of Carnguwch is included. And his fame spread significantly further than north Wales. There are dedications, too, in Powys at Berriew, in Monmouthshire in Llanveynoe (appropriately enough for border-country Monmouthshire, this is a part-English, part-Welsh version of 'Llan Feuno'), and, most surprisingly, in Somerset at Culbone – *Cil Beuno* (literally, 'Beuno's retreat'). Nevertheless, Beuno is inescapably the saint of north Wales, linked historically – and, indeed, miraculously – from Holywell in the east to Clynnog Fawr in the west. St Winifride's Well at Holywell is said to have sprung up at the spot where Winifride's head hit the ground when she was beheaded by Caradoc for refusing his advances. Beuno, who was Winifride's uncle, restored her to life, and was rewarded with a yearly gift of an embroidered garment that would be dropped into the well in Holywell and be carried on the water, unharmed, to the well at Clynnog Fawr. Like all patron saints of great antiquity stories of his miraculous powers abound.

He was also famously a Welsh patriot. In their book, *The Lives of the Saints*, Baring-Gould and Fisher relate the story of Beuno walking with his followers near the Severn and, on hearing the hunting cries of an Englishman across the river, told his followers they should 'leave this place for the nation of the man with the strange tongue, whose cry I heard beyond the river urging on his hounds, will invade this place and it will be theirs, and they will hold it as their possession'. The mother church at Clynnog Fawr is dedicated to Beuno as is the little hospice church at Pistyll (Walk 10).

The walks are designed so that, wherever possible, the walker comes upon the ancient *llan* at some midway point, stumbling upon it as if by chance. These churches do not announce themselves from afar, in the manner of the classic English village church, its spire pointing confidently heavenwards. They crouch, rather, hug the ground, drawing the eye not upwards to a world beyond but downwards, into the earth itself. The Celtic tradition, its poetry and its piety, places an emphasis on the indivisibility of God and Nature. These verses from a ninth-century Irish poem could easily be by one of Beuno's followers some 300 years earlier, standing at the summit of Yr Eifl, seeing the glint of water amongst the trees far below on the plain, his hopes and his spirit soaring after the arduous climb:

> O Son of the living God
> ancient, eternal king,
> grant me a hidden hut
> to be my home in the wild,
> with green shallow water
> running by its side,
> and a clear pool to wash off sin
> by grace of the Holy Ghost;
> a lovely church, with linen,
> a home for Heaven's King,
> with bright lamps shining down
> on the clear bright Scriptures

Llŷn is rich in places where the ancient past seems as present as the ground beneath your feet. When you walk in Llŷn you do so in the company of those spirited wanderers whose presence haunts the landscape still. R. S. Thomas put it like this:

> These very seas
> are baptised. The parish
> has a saint's name time cannot
> unfrock.

The ancient footprint of Christianity in Wales is vividly evident in the holy wells found across the peninsula and in the inscribed stones dating from the fifth to the ninth centuries. The stones are of two main types: the fifth/sixth-century inscribed memorial stones and the seventh/ninth-century cross-incised stones found in certain of the churchyards but, more often, on roadsides, like the stone on the road at Pistyll (Walk 10). The wheeled cross at Capel Uchaf above Clynnog Fawr is a particularly striking example of these ancient wayside objects.

There are several spectacular examples of the even earlier memorial stones on the peninsula, not least the 'Veracius' and 'Senacus' memorials at St Hywyn's in Aberdaron (Walk 13), and the monumental slabs from Llangwnnadl, now in the entrance hall at Plas Glyn y Weddw (Walk 4). In Llanaelhaearn (Walk 8) the fifth-century 'Melitus stone', green with lichen, stands in the churchyard, only yards from the road. There is a unique inscription on a fifth/sixth- century stone in the pretty village of Llangian. The Latin inscription, in vertical script, translates as 'of Melus, the Doctor, son of Martinus. He lies'. This is the only early Christian stone in Britain which records the life of a 'medicus', doctor. Should you visit Llangian it is worth noting that the key to the tiny church is held at the village shop.

Pilgrimage in the Middle Ages
Bardsey's importance as a pilgrim destination was significantly

enhanced early in the twelfth century when Pope Calixtus famously decreed that three pilgrimages to the island were equivalent to one to Rome. Throughout the Middle Ages pilgrims making their way to the holy 'Island of the Saints' would have thronged the trackways, 'coffin roads' and sea-lanes of the peninsula until the Dissolution of the Monasteries brought an abrupt end to pilgrimage and traditional piety. The thirteenth-century Abbey of St Mary on Bardsey was dissolved and its buildings destroyed in 1537. Only part of the tower still remains.

Evidence for the scale of pilgrim traffic is dramatically provided by the extraordinary St Beuno's church at Clynnog Fawr. Relative to the modest churches throughout Llŷn, St Beuno's seems to belong to another place altogether, its squat grandeur a shock when seen for the first time, as if the hollow in which it sits were due to that great weight of stone. John Leland notes pithily that 'Clunnock Vawr in Arvon (is) a great parish, and the fairest chirch yn al Caernarvonshire as better than Bangor.'

The present church was built in the late fifteenth century, perhaps less than 100 years before Leland's visit, and was substantially funded by the donations of the pilgrims making their way to Bardsey along the northern route from Bangor. It is an irony of epic proportions that the Reformation and the sudden end of pilgrimage came within a few years of the completion of this extravagant building programme. St Beuno's is often referred to as a mother church, a term particular to the traditions and organisation of early Celtic Christianity. It is tempting and pleasing to think of St Beuno's as a mother in a less technical sense, an ample and generous presence on the edge of Caernarfon Bay, looking out for her little brood scattered along the slender length of the peninsula.

Though I do not include a walk to the formidable St Beuno's in Clynnog Fawr, the reader interested as much in the churches as in the walks should set time aside to visit the church that T. J.

Hughes dubs 'the medieval spiritual powerhouse of Western Arfon'. The walks in this book feature churches that are altogether different: simple, mainly single-chamber buildings, as plain and functional as the old stone barns and byres that typify the predominantly agricultural landscape of Llŷn.

Though the walks are self-contained and can be done in any order I have grouped them so that they follow the general direction of these old pilgrim routes. The first six walks follow the southern route from Treflys in *Eifionydd* to Pen Llŷn. The next six follow the northern route from Llanfaglan in *Arfon* to Pen Llŷn. The final walk, under the heading, 'Journey's End', is the walk around the headland at Pen Llŷn where the majesty and mystery of Bardsey, or Ynys Enlli – 'the island in treacherous waters' – comes suddenly into view.

I should just say that the 'Pilgrim Trail' signs found at or near some of the churches on the peninsula do not indicate trails in the usual sense of a system of marked footpaths but rather indicate the importance of a particular church in relation to medieval pilgrimage. The actual routes those pilgrims took are now largely a matter of conjecture, the old trackways lost beneath tarmac or buildings or farmland. Nevertheless, understanding the relationship of a particular church to these ancient routes and traditions transforms one's experience of it.

Language and Landscape

As we have seen, this landscape is permeated with the lore and language of the early Christian church. Once the principle of the *llan* and associated saint's name is understood this should prevent no difficulty to the non-Welsh speaker. The vast number of names for topographical features – *afon* (river), *mynydd* (hill, mountain), *coed* (wood), for example – will prove more challenging, not to mention those adjectives built into place-names – *mawr/fawr* (great or big), *uchaf* (higher or upper), *isaf* (lower), *hen* (old), for example. Of particular interest here are those place-name qualifiers that derive directly from medieval pilgrimage, for example, *cae esteddfa* (literally, 'resting field'), as in the fields at St Beuno's in Pistyll and St Gwynhoedl's in Llangwnnadl.

In addition to those words that are part of place-names there are two Welsh common nouns that are used throughout the book. These are *llan* (and its plural, *llannau*) and *clawdd*, which I always couple with 'bank'. *Llan*, as we have seen, is key to the physical and cultural topography of Wales as a whole. The other term, *clawdd* bank, may not be unique to Llŷn but is an important, even a defining, feature of the landscape. *Clawdd* banks, those field-boundary walls of stone and earth invariably ablaze with flowers in season, are as characteristic of Llŷn as the towering hedges are of Devon. Many are medieval in origin, as in the ancient fields of Uwchmynydd at the western tip of the peninsula. The elaborately constructed *clawdd* banks between Aberdesach and Llanaelhaearn, on the other hand, were built as part of the multi-million pound reconstruction of the A499 completed in 2010. The Llŷn Peninsula West map shows a feature between Mynytho and Llangian called 'Y Clawdd Mawr' – 'the great *clawdd* bank'. This, like several other such banks, is also a public footpath, although progress through the shoulder-high bracken is not easy. Throughout, italics are used not only for *llan* and *clawdd* but any other specific Welsh terms for which there is no adequate or attractive enough translation, *englyn*, for example, and its plural, *englynion*. The *englyn* is an ancient Welsh poetic form, as strict and compressed as Japanese *haiku*. The word that you will encounter on all of the walks, of course, is *eglwys*, church.

And then, of course, there's the pronunciation which, despite the panic of non-Welsh speakers, is simple and phonetic once the pronunciation of the alphabet has been grasped. I should point out, here, that the frequently occurring *Beuno* is pronounced, roughly, 'Bayno', and not at all like the confusingly similar-looking Spanish word 'bueno'. The apparently consonant-heavy *eglwys* is a mellifluous-sounding word pronounced 'eggloowees'. I strongly recommend that you acquire one of the Welsh primers available in all local bookshops. Knowledge of the language, however scant, will immeasurably enrich your experience of walking on the peninsula and visiting its churches.

Wildlife and wildflowers
Though not the focus of this book the wildflowers constitute one of the greatest pleasures of walking the hills, plains and coasts of Llŷn. The landscape is vibrant with colour and movement from early spring to late autumn, from the delicate pink of lady's smock at Carreg y Llam in early spring to the startling bog cotton high on Yr Eifl's slopes in summer, its seed heads like tufts of wool snagged from passing sheep, to the pink pincushions of thrift covering the ancient pasture and *clawdd* banks of Uwchmynydd. The lanes of inland Llŷn are a particular delight too, the hedgerows and verges a riot of changing colour, from the yellows of primrose and cowslip in spring to the reds and purples of summer with its spires of foxgloves and the gracefully waving red campion. The blaze of heather and gorse are the glory of the high hillsides from midsummer to autumn. For each of the walks I give a brief indication of some of the wildflowers you might expect to see at certain times of the year.

Llŷn is famous for its wildlife, in particular its marine mammals and its colonies of breeding seabirds. Much of the peninsula is a designated Area of Outstanding Natural Beauty (AONB), the purpose of which is to protect and promote the landscape itself but, equally, the wildlife sustained by it. There are, in addition, two Areas of Special Scientific Interest (SSSIs) – the inland wetlands of Cors Geirch and the coastal Pen Llŷn a'r Sarnau. There are also various nature reserves (including the imaginative Lon Cob Bach in the middle of Pwllheli) and the serene Foryd Bay (Walk 7), bird sanctuaries like Carreg y Llam (Walk 10), and sections of Heritage Coast like Morfa (Walk 8) and Braich y Pwll (Walk 13), all of which ensure that the habitats that sustain the astonishing diversity of wildlife on the peninsula are protected. But for those wanting to experience the range of marine wildlife it is, appropriately enough, Bardsey that is the Holy Grail.

Bardsey

The yellow catamaran taking its handful of passengers from Porth Meudwy to Bardsey cruises alongside the cliff wall of Mynydd Enlli, the island's eastern edge, the skipper pointing out the sea-birds on the ledges and in the water, on the cliff-tops and in the cave-mouths, as the boat slowly approaches the island's only landing spot, where the seals loll and honk noisily. The skipper's mother, the poet and island resident Christine Evans, says this of the sea-birds congregating on Mynydd Enlli:

> Herring gulls and black-backed gulls loiter in casual groups above the densely-populated ledges where guillemot and razorbill throng on their stacked ledges, for they like to nest almost wing to wing. Fulmars tuck their single egg into a notch or crevice at a height from which they can sail majestically out over the waves, surfing the air currents without so much as a flap. Kittiwakes wawl and mewl and flap about. Puffins have recently colonised the softer ground between the stones of the boulder scree, ten pairs now, despite the vigilant presence of the peregrine falcon and his mate.

In the same book, *Bardsey*, she makes reference to an extraordinary natural feature on the more sheltered south-west side of the island:

> All the springs rise on this gentler side, from a fold of limestone deep within the rock, an aquifer that, it is claimed, runs from St Mary's Well on the mainland under the Sound to rise two miles and two hundred feet higher on Bardsey. Once, Ernest watched in awe as a water diviner directed the

boat along the flow of fresh water by the energy in the metal rods he held in each hand, thrumming and dipping in response through a hundred fathoms of salt.

If we are prepared to enter into the spirit of this uncommon place, where the miraculous and the mundane are routinely and inextricably entwined, the story of this limestone aquifer becomes a powerful metaphor connecting the natural and the sacred, the island and the mainland, the medieval and the contemporary pilgrim.

With all this talk of signs and wonders you may think it a relief to turn to 'Enlli', Harri Webb's charmingly acerbic poem that begins:

> No, I've never been there, with luck never shall,
> Would be bored stiff in five minutes. All islands
> Of this size are horribly alike, fit only
> For sheep, saints and lighthousekeepers.

But Ynys Enlli – 'the island in the treacherous current' – this 'illusion anchored in rock', as Harri Webb calls it, continues to fascinate. A millennium and a half since Cadfan and his companions built their *llan* on the island, Bardsey still draws pilgrims of one kind or another, but it is to the natural world that they look for inspiration rather than to the frankly slightly dispiriting remains of the thirteenth-century abbey. But then this is entirely at one with the ancient history of Llŷn and those founding fathers of the Celtic Church who sought solitude in nature in order to be at one with their God. And, as we have seen, these wanderers were also the founding fathers of Wales itself. Harri Webb concludes his poem:

> If anybody prints this poem I'll send the price of it
> To the fund to acquire Enlli for the nation.
> God damn it, it is the Nation.

Access to the churches

In each of the walk descriptions I indicate whether the church is generally open or kept locked. In the latter case I recommend that you contact the Diocesan Centre in Bangor on 01248 353983 to arrange access via the local key-holder. The key for St Engan's (Walk 5) is held behind the bar in the local, very welcoming pub, The Sun Inn.

WALKS ON THE SOUTHERN PILGRIM ROUTE

WALK 1

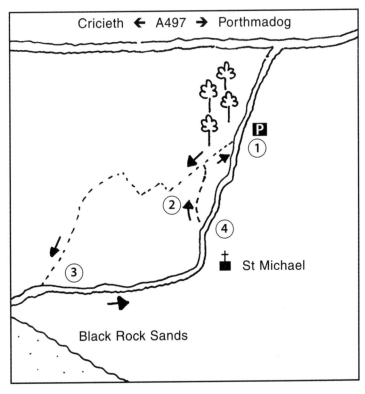

Cricieth ← A497 → Porthmadog

P
①

②

④

†
■ St Michael

③

Black Rock Sands

St Michael, Treflys

WALK 1
St Michael, Treflys

From the churchyard look down upon Cardigan Bay
and the pilgrim route from Tywyn and St David's

Landscape	Ancient woodland, rough pasture and the famous Black Rock Sands
Distance	About two miles
Difficulty	Moderate
Time	Allow two hours
Suggested map	OS Explorer 254, Llŷn Peninsula East
Start/finish	Grid reference: SH 536385
Parking	From the A497 turn at Coed y Chwarel onto the lane next to the railway bridge. After about a mile park at the little pull-in near the start of the signed footpath through the woods
Facilities	There are no public toilets or refreshment facilities en route
Wildflowers	In spring the banks are studded with garlic mustard, or jack-by-the-hedge, whilst the delicate wood-sorrel carpets the shadier wooded areas.

The Walk

On this relatively short walk you pass through a bewildering variety of terrain: ancient woodlands, rough grazing edged with tumbledown stone walls, secluded farmland, and after a short but sharp climb, you find yourself in a churchyard on a ridge high above the northern tip of Cardigan Bay. As you leave the churchyard the views rival anywhere on the peninsula: behind you, to the south, the great sweep of Cardigan Bay; on your left, Criccieth Castle, its jagged, romantic outline sharp against the western sky; due north, the Snowdon massif; and, to your right, the incomparable Meirionydd mountains, from the Rhinogydd to the majestic Cader Idris.

Directions

1   Head up the track through the woods and over the charming little stone bridge and make for the iron gate pretty much straight ahead. Go through the gate and head up the field, keeping to the wall on your right. Continue, over some informal stone steps, until you reach the iron gate in the wall on your right.

2   Go through this gate and straight ahead down a couple of old stone steps then go left. Continue straight ahead and cross the wall beneath the massive and low-spreading tree. Only twenty or so paces from the wall bear right along the grassy track leading towards the open farm gate. Go through then head left, keeping the farm on your right. Go through the next farm gate and onto the wide dirt track, past the evocative remains of an old tree house. At the end of the track follow the yellow arrow up a green path, through a wooden gate, and into a large field. Keep to the left as you descend towards the farm at the bottom, just before which you go through the gate onto the lane.

3   Turn left on the lane and begin the short ascent. Shortly before the crest of the hill the bell-cote of St Michael's comes into view, as do the distant mountains to the south and east From the churchyard turn right onto the road. Moel y Gest is now on your right, Snowdonia straight ahead, and to your left, Cricieth castle seems to float above the sea.

4   Follow the first footpath sign on your left, using the farm gate a little further on rather than the rusting, precarious one next to the sign. Make your way across the field to the iron gate in the bottom left-hand corner. Go through the gate, rejoin the path over the little bridge and return to your car.

The Church

SH 534378

Access: The church is kept locked.

Given the proximity – in the summer months – of caravans in the neighbouring field, this is not the most isolated of the churches, but it is quite possibly the most exposed. From the sloping, south side of the churchyard, looking out at the dizzying views of the sea below and Snowdonia behind, St Michael's feels more like a lookout post or coastguard station. And from here there is a direct view of the southern pilgrim route heading down the west coast to St David's. It is said that from the abbey at Tywyn, twenty miles or so south of Treflys, St Cadfan first saw Bardsey and decided to build his *llan* and his community there.

Despite the busy summer world of Black Rock Sands it is easy enough – particularly in the winter – to imagine the austere Early Medieval life of this church. Unusually, there is no

Looking towards Meirionnydd

Looking towards Snowdon

running water nearby but the alignment of its oval *llan* in the landscape, its simultaneous views of sea and mountain, both immediate and distant, is as good an example of the ancient Celtic tradition as any of the churches in Llŷn.

Much of the visible structure of the church dates from Victorian renovations, but it still has that barn-like, rough-hewn simplicity evocative of a much earlier era. Rust from the bell stains the west wall, and from the bell-cote the rope-pull dangles as if from an old harbour wall; an apt enough association in a spot where the sea has traditionally dominated community life and continues to do so, even if fishing boats have been exchanged for pleasure craft.

The oldest part of the existing structure is probably fourteenth century. Striking and dramatic evidence of the presence of St Michael's in the earliest days of Celtic Christianity can be found in the sixth-century inscribed stone inside the church, which is, according to the Diocesan Directory of Open Churches, one of only seven such stones in Britain.

The view towards Moel y Gest from the lane aat Treflys

WALK 2

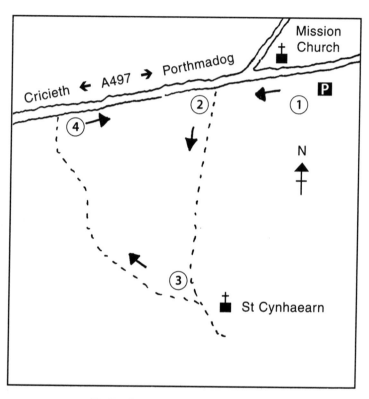

St Cynhaearn, Ynyscynhaearn

St Cynhaearn, Ynyscynhaearn

The island church no longer on an island

Landscape	Rough pasture and drained marshland
Distance	About three miles
Difficulty	Easy
Time	Allow two hours
Suggested map	OS Explorer 254 Llŷn Peninsula East
Start/finish	Grid reference: SH 527397
Parking	In the car park of *Y Ganolfan* (the community centre) just outside Pentrefelin on the A497
Facilities	There are no public toilets or refreshment facilities en route
Wildflowers	Gorse dots the rocky hills to the west, seeming to flower at almost all times of the year though at its best in late summer. In spring the banks are studded with the white stars of greater stitchwort, or in Welsh, *bara can a llaeth*, 'white bread and milk'.

The Walk

It is hard to believe, walking between the noble trees flanking the old causeway from Pentrefelin, that the busy main road to Porthmadog is only a few hundred metres behind you or, indeed, that the popular Black Rock Sands is less than a mile ahead of you. But this is not the remoteness of those isolated churches in the northern mountains. This is the remoteness of the secluded garden. And that is how the church appears when you first spot it: like a plain but pleasing country house in a modest walled garden, old trees sheltering it from the wind off the sea. You climb the rise from the wooded dell at Bron-y-Gadair Farm, with its confusion of trickling brooks and streams,

Approaching the church

and there, as you emerge from the trees, is the church, perhaps half a mile away. To your left the lush pasture slopes gently away towards the woodland and the appealingly odd, conical tip of Moel-y-Gest. To your right the rough moorland rises sharply towards Moel-y-Gadair where sheep pause momentarily to stare as they amble between gorse and rocky outcrops. Ahead of you Craig Ddu stands sentinel over Black Rock Sands.

Directions
1 Turn left out of the car park and walk towards the village.
2 Just before the first house on the left hand side of the road go through the field gate on your left. Head straight down the tarmac roadway. Continue along the lane, through heavily wooded country, which eventually opens out at the top of the rise after the brook. To your left rich green fields sweep down towards the drained marsh, the peaks of Snowdon (*Yr Wyddfa*) magnificent in the distance, and to your right, the

rough moorland rises sharply. It is from here that you catch your first glimpses of the church, sitting snug within its *llan*, tall trees sheltering it from the wind off the sea. From here it could easily be a modest farmhouse. Follow the causeway over the bridge and up to the lych gate with its reference to 'Jack Black, Ystumllyn', memorialised on his headstone less colourfully as plain 'John Ystumllyn'.

3   To return head back down the causeway, and just after the bridge climb the stone steps up to the very attractive iron gate into the field. Keep to the left as you head across the field to the kissing gate. Cross the stone slabs to the permanently open gateway by the now step-less stile. Continue straight ahead through the middle of the field, between two little rocky outcrops, through another open gateway and on to the stile in the hedge alongside the A497.

4   Turn right and walk through Pentrefelin and back to the car park.

The west door

39

North side of the churchyard

The Church
SH 525388
Access: The church is kept locked.

The original *llan* is believed to have been founded early in the seventh century by Cynhaearn, the brother of Aelhaearn, and a follower of Beuno. Ynyscynhaearn means 'St Cynhaearn's Island', and this church was once perched above the surrounding waters of Lake Ystumllyn, making it both an inland and an island church. The lake was drained in the nineteenth century, and the late Georgian church is now surrounded only by its stone wall and the grazing sheep that often wander in through the lych gate and keep down the marshy grass that would otherwise overwhelm the little churchyard.

All that now remains of the twelfth-century stone church that would have replaced the original timber structure is the nave. The north and south transepts were both added in the

1600s, and the strikingly plain exterior that we see today is the outcome of the complete rebuild carried out in 1830, albeit in the style of the previous century.

The church itself is unmistakeably Georgian in style as is the uncompromisingly rectilinear churchyard that contains the graves of two men whose lives afford a fascinating insight into Welsh life in the eighteenth century. David Owen, or Dafydd y Garreg Wen, the harpist and composer, died in 1741 at the age of twenty-nine. He was from a local farm, Garreg Wen (*carreg:* rock; *gwen/gwyn*: white), and in the Welsh manner was known by his place of birth. His best-known piece, supposedly composed on his death bed, and also known as 'Dafydd y Garreg Wen', was given an arrangement by Haydn and has become a staple of the Welsh folk music canon.

The other notable grave is of a figure whose life spanned the second half of the eighteenth century. 'Jack Black Ystumllyn' was a black servant in the household of the wealthy Wynne family. It is believed he was captured as a young child, possibly in Africa, by a member of the family in the 1740s. A servant rather than a slave, he worked as a gardener for the family, became fluent in both English and Welsh, clearly enjoyed much popularity with the local people, and eventually married a local girl with whom he had seven children. He died about 1790 and is said to have admitted on his deathbed that he had, on occasion, played his fiddle on the Sabbath. His memorial leans against a far grander tomb. It is a simple stone but with a touching *englyn*, now almost indecipherable, that reads:

Yn India gynna'm ganwyd – a nghamrau
Yng Nghymru'm bedyddiwyd;
Wele'r fan dan lechan lwyd
Du oeraidd y'm daearwyd

> [India was the land of my birth
> But I was baptised in Wales;

This spot, marked by a grey slate
Is my cold, dark resting place]

There is no 'Jack Black' on the headstone. Here his name is given as 'John Ystumllyn'.

The Mission Church
Shortly before the car park, on the opposite side of the road, the Mission Church stands behind trees a little way back from the main road. It dates from the 1930s, and its highly distinctive bell tower was designed by the creator of Portmeirion, Clough Williams-Ellis. The church was built as a more accessible alternative for the villagers than the remote St Cynhaearn's, where his wife, Rachel Williams-Ellis, was a churchwarden for many years. The modern Mission Church now looks far more abandoned and forlorn than any of the ancient churches of Llŷn.

Jack Ystumllyn headstone

WALK 3

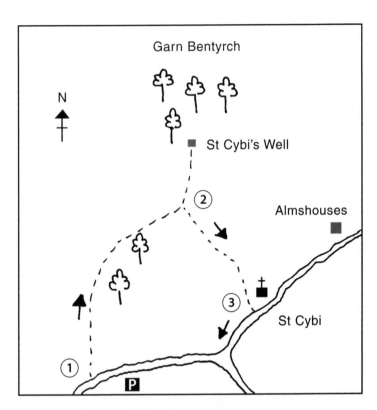

Garn Bentyrch

N

St Cybi's Well

Almshouses

St Cybi

St Cybi. Llangybi

St Cybi, Llangybi

The paradox of a holy well that is both ancient and modern

Landscape	A peaceful wooded valley beneath the rugged Garn Bentyrch
Distance	About a mile and a half
Difficulty	Easy
Time	Allow an hour and a half
Suggested map	OS Explorer 254 Llŷn Peninsula East
Start/finish	Grid reference: SH 427411
Parking	There is a small parking space alongside the kissing-gate and heritage sign for Ffynnon Gybi. Alternatively there is usually space in the village near the church.
Facilities	There are no public toilets or refreshment facilities en route.
Wildflowers	In the hedgerows dog violet in early spring and red campion and garlic mustard as summer approaches. Mighty hardwood trees up on the lower slopes of Garn Bentyrch. Meadowsweet in summer in the niches of the well itself.

The Walk

Near the church is a fine chalybeate spring, called Ffynnon Gybi, inclosed with a stone wall, having stone seats around it; the water was formerly in great repute for its efficacy in the cure of scorbutic complaints, and is still found beneficial in chronic cases. On the summit of Garn Pentyrch, or Garn Llangybi, a high conical hill, is a very extensive and perfect ancient British encampment.

Samuel Lewis, A Topographical Dictionary of Wales, *1849*

Garn Bentyrch to the north

There is an extraordinary number of holy wells on the peninsula, Gwynedd County Council listing some fifty in the area west of the A487. Many of these are in a poor state of repair. Many, indeed, are difficult to see at all without fighting a dispiriting battle with bramble, bracken and nettles. Many of them are little more than a hole in the ground, albeit edged in stone. Ffynnon Cybi, however, is of a very different order. Here there is a well complex consisting of three buildings: the walled well-chamber itself, the adjoining cottage, and a short walk downstream of the well, a stone-built latrine. The adjoining cottage would have provided accommodation for the custodian of the well and for the pilgrims seeking cures for their ailments.

Whilst the well is of ancient origin, no doubt with pre-Christian ritual significance, the sturdy stone buildings that you can see were erected in the early 1700s and represent the focus not so much of medieval piety as of eighteenth-century medical fashion. The 'scorbutic complaints' that Samuel Lewis mentions were a very eighteenth-century preoccupation as, indeed, was the attachment to the curative powers of 'chalybeate' or sulphuric waters. However incongruous it might seem to make any sort of connection between these little, rough stone buildings and the elegant crescents of Cheltenham and Bath, Ffynnon Cybi, in the early eighteenth century, was a spa. It seems that the man behind this development was William Price of Rhiwlas, a nephew of the Royalist landowner, Charles Jones who, in 1640, endowed the exquisite almshouses in the village that you will see later in the walk.

Inside the main well-chamber there is a series of large niches set into the walls. I have heard it suggested that these would have housed statues of the saints and the Virgin Mary, in the manner of a medieval church. Would this have been likely in a spa, however tiny, in eighteenth-century, Protestant Wales? This is one of the many puzzles one encounters on this intriguing short walk. Standing at the water's edge, inside this chamber, one is acutely aware of the contradictory strands of faith and science, magic and medicine, woven into its long history. The ghosts of its miraculous and rational pasts vie for our attention. In 2010 I happened upon a 'Youth Mission' from Bethnal Green here at the well. As the young people clambered over the ruins of the custodian's cottage and teetered on its roofless walls, their adult leaders sat on the stone seats in the well-chamber, their bare feet submerged in the alarmingly green and brackish waters of the well, extemporising prayers for spiritual guidance and healing.

However busy this place must once have been, whether with medieval penitents or scrofulous eighteenth-century patients, this pretty valley at the foot of Garn Bentyrch is now a wonderfully calm and peaceful place.

If you would like to extend the walk and build in some stiff, physical challenge, you should visit the 'perfect ancient British encampment' before making your way to the church. The climb up the 'high conical hill' of Garn Bentyrch starts at the gate immediately behind the well. Simply follow the recently installed way markers through the series of gates to the trig point at the summit. The inner, early medieval ring of the Iron Age hillfort is less well preserved today than it was when Samuel Lewis was assiduously making his notes in the early years of the nineteenth century.

Directions

1   From the kissing-gate head straight down the hill and through the next gate. Continue ahead beneath the spreading branches of the large and varied trees where the cattle gather on hot days. At the point where the path clearly divides into an upper and a lower path go between the enormous stones onto the lower path and make your way alongside the very pretty brook to the entrance to the well with its information board.

2   To walk to the church go straight ahead at the entrance gate and onto the steep path immediately opposite. Go over the stone stile into the field and make for the steps in the bottom right-hand corner of the churchyard wall.

3   To return to your car turn right out of the lychgate and right again at the T-junction. To see the beautiful seventeenth-century almshouses turn left out of the gate. The almshouses are about hundred metres along the road.

The Church
SH 428412
Access: The church is kept locked

After visiting the well you will walk up old stone steps between gorse and blackberry bushes, across a field, and up even older steps into the churchyard of St Cybi, where you will find a cross-incised sixth-century stone, green with lichen, propped unceremoniously against the shady north wall of the lychgate, as if left there by an absent-minded sexton gone home for the day. The churchyards of Llŷn abound in unannounced, understated marvels such as this.

South porch

Cross-incised stone

Looking outwards from the well

WALK 4

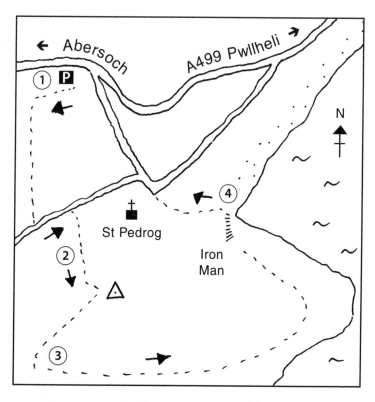

St Pedrog, Llanbedrog

St Pedrog, Llanbedrog

The church dedicated to the Welshman
who was to become Cornwall's most famous saint

Landscape	Coastal headland
Distance	About three miles
Difficulty	Moderate
Time	Allow three hours
Suggested map	OS Explorer 253, Llŷn Peninsula West
Start/finish	Grid reference: SH 328318
Parking	In the car park of the Glyn-y-Weddw pub or in the larger car park to one side of the Londis store next to the pub
Facilities	Café and public toilets at Plas Glyn-y-Weddw
Wildflowers	Celandines, bluebells and wood anemone in spring on the lower, wooded slopes; spectacular heathers in summer up on the headland

The Walk

Mynydd Tir-y-Cwmwd is at the seaward end of the chain of volcanic hills that forms the eastern border of the Cors Geirch wetlands. At its northern head is Garn Fadryn, the majestic, all-seeing presence at the very centre of Llŷn. St Tudwal's Islands (*Ynysoedd Tudwal*) lie tantalisingly close a mile or so to the south of the headland. St Tudwal's Island East (*Ynys Tudwal Fach*) is believed to be the site of the sixth-century hermitage of St Tudwal, another of those formidable Breton holy men that roamed Wales in the fifth to the seventh centuries seeking both solitude and followers. The remains of a priory, mentioned in the 1291 tax rolls, is the only surviving evidence of a medieval presence on the island. The remote mystery of these islands in

On the eastern edge of Mynydd Tir-y-Cwmwd

the ancient seaway of St Tudwal's Road is tempered somewhat by the knowledge that the east island's current owner, a latter-day missionary of sorts, is the TV writer and animal rights campaigner, Carla Lane. The west island (*Ynys Tudwal Fawr*), with its still-functioning Victorian lighthouse, is now a holiday home owned by the celebrity adventurer, Bear Grylls.

Pwllheli lies to the east, and the town's West End beach is separated from Llanbedrog only at low tide. Though divided only by a small, rocky outcrop, the two beaches could hardly be more different: the forlorn West End with its muddy dunes exposed to the full force of the prevailing wind, and Llanbedrog's tree-fringed, sheltered beach, its gaily-coloured beach huts lending this old fishing village a hint of genteel Frinton-on-Sea or well-heeled Southwold. The Victorian entrepreneur Solomon Andrews made an ultimately ill-starred attempt to link Pwllheli and Llanbedrog with a horse-drawn tramway that ran more or less smoothly from 1896 until it was washed away only thirty-odd years later by a particularly fierce sea in 1927. The large houses of Pwllheli's West End, visible from the headland, are also part of his legacy, as is the magnificent, gothic Plas Glyn y Weddw (*plas*: mansion; *glyn*: valley; *gweddw*: widow), the old dower house of the Love Parry Jones family, that Andrews bought in 1892, and that is now the rather beautiful gallery and arts centre, Oriel Plas Glyn y Weddw. In the entrance porch are two important sixth-century memorial stones recovered from an early Christian grave at Penprys Farm, Llannor, in the early nineteenth century. They were removed to the Ashmolean Museum in Oxford in 1885 and not returned to Llŷn until 1993. You will want to visit Plas Glyn y Weddw for these extraordinary ancient monuments as well as for the art gallery, shop and attractive café.

From the garden at Plas Glyn y Weddw you will notice a figure high up on the headland, a figure that often appears to be moving against the scudding clouds. This figure is The Iron Man, a rust-coloured exoskeleton who stares impassively out to sea, the wind careening through his open ribcage and his ancient warrior's helmet of a face. He is the second replacement for the wooden ship's figurehead placed there by Solomon Andrews. I met a villager on the headland who had been involved in the relatively recent installation of the Iron Man. He and a handful of volunteers had built the concrete base, carrying up from the beach – a bucket at a time – the sand and stone for its construction. Think about the enormity of that task when you descend the 200 or so steep, irregular steps as they twist and turn down the wooded slopes to the sea. Juddering down these steps it is all too easy to imagine that alarming figure from the cliff top clanking down behind you, slowly but surely closing the gap.

Directions

1 Walk down to the pub and turn right onto the lane separating the beer garden from the pub. Continue along the

lane and turn left at the T junction with the old footpath sign. Follow the footpath till the road then turn left and almost immediately right onto the path at the sign for Tir-y-Cymwd. Climb the path to the wooded lane. From here there are spectacular views to the south-east over Cardigan Bay, and to the north-west, of Garn Fadryn, the mountain at the head of the line of hills ending here at the headland.

2   Go through the waymarked gate, up the run of stone steps, and continue up the steep but short climb through the woods, eventually emerging into the heather, gorse and close-cropped grass of the headland. Continue straight ahead towards the rough cairn and the seating area with its depiction on slate of the mountains of Gwynedd. Turn right and head for the trig point and, from here, take the left-hand fork. The Warren, Abersoch, St Tudwal's Islands are all in full view as you descend towards the house at Mount Pleasant to your right.

3   At the green T-junction go left and follow the fairly obvious footpath closest to the sea. For a dramatic, if dangerous, view of the cliffs and the old quarry workings, take a right onto a little path marked by a sturdy wooden pole and an old iron bedstead. Take great care when approaching the cliff edge. Continue following the outline of the headland: at times over stone and rock but, mainly, on obvious paths through the heather, until you come upon the strange and improbable Iron Man. Continue towards the steps down to the beach.

4   Go left onto the causeway, past the boat house and the impossibly pretty cottage, Foxhole, with its imposing large chimneys. Continue onto the lane, Lon Nant Iago, that leads up from the beach to Plas Glyn y Weddw and the church. To return to your car go left out of the church and immediately left up the hill to the Glyn y Weddw pub.

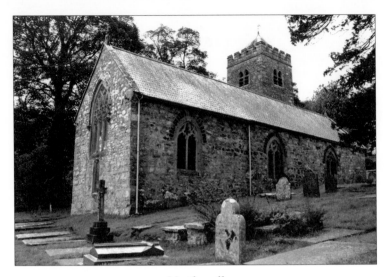

North wall

The Church
SH 329315
Access: Open throughout the year during daylight hours.

St Pedrog's sits snugly in the densely wooded 'Widow's Glen', protected from the winds off the sea. The raised, curvilinear *llan* and the stream running alongside its southern boundary are the only obvious clues to its sixth-century origins. The church was restored and given a tower in the Victorian years but the thirteenth-century nave exudes a powerful sense of medieval piety. In the windows there is some pre-Reformation glass, and this single-chamber church seems always to be filled with a crepuscular glow. The font is fifteenth century.

WALK 5

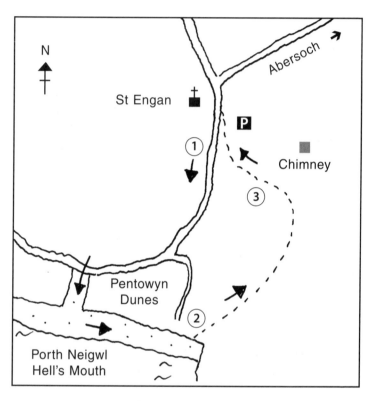

N

St Engan

Abersoch

P

Chimney

①

③

②

Pentowyn
Dunes

Porth Neigwl
Hell's Mouth

St Engan, Llanengan

St Engan, Llanengan

*The final stopping-off point for pilgrims
following the southern route to Bardsey*

Landscape	Exposed coast and sheltered marshy plain
Distance	About four miles
Difficulty	Moderate
Time	Allow a good three hours
Suggested map	OS Explorer 253 Llŷn Peninsula West
Start/finish	Grid reference: SH 294270
Parking	Park at The Sun Inn about a hundred metres from the church
Facilities	The Sun Inn. There are no public toilets en route.
Wildflowers	According to Buglife, The Invertebrate Conservation Trust, Porth Neigwl is 'the most important site in Wales for soft cliff invertebrates' and 'one of only two sites in the UK that support populations of the endangered mason bee'. On these soft cliffs can also be found the bright yellow pompoms of colts foot in very early spring, the intriguingly lacy wild carrot – also known as Queen Anne's Lace – and the gorse-like flower of the common birds foot trefoil whose buttery yellow blooms last from May to August.

The Walk

The elemental power concentrated in the perfect bay of Porth Neigwl (or, more graphically, 'Hell's Mouth') is overwhelming, even on a calm summer's day. In the winter, the breakers slowly unfurl along the full four miles of sand, the vast rumble of the waves often indistinguishable from the sky-splitting roar of the fighter planes from RAF Valley frequently on exercises over these waters.

Once beyond the dunes and onto the splashy grass the quieter drama of the plain slowly asserts itself. The large-scale field boundaries of the nineteenth-century farms obscure the medieval origins of Neigwl. This area, from the lower slopes of Mynydd Rhiw in the west to the Llanengan escarpment in the east, formed the *maerdref*, or Royal Township, of the lords of the commote of Cymydmaen. There is no record of the whereabouts of the *llys*, or princely palace, or, indeed, any obvious physical indicators of the area's antiquity and importance. But something of its medieval status inheres in the place-names, particularly those farmhouse names indicative of the gradual parcelling up of a medieval township into private ownership – Plas Neigwl, Neigwl Uchaf, Neigwl Ganol. There are, apparently, references in Elizabethan legal texts to the Manor of Neigwl, and in the Wynn of Gwydir papers of around 1620, Neigwl is referred to as 'Crown Land'.

More obvious, as you approach Llanengan itself, is the more recent history of nineteenth-century lead mining in the area. At Tan-yr-Allt the chimney arising directly from the grassy ridge to your right is startling evidence of the industry that drove the economy here in the second half of the nineteenth century. At one point nine of the ten houses comprising Bay View Terrace were occupied by miners and their families, the majority of them from elsewhere, in particular Cornwall, Shropshire and Meirionydd.

Directions

1   From the car park turn left onto the lane. As you head down the lane note the chimney up on the escarpment to your left, all that remains of the Tan-yr-Allt lead mines. The Neigwl plain stretches away to your right, the wooded, lower slopes

of Plas yn Rhiw rising at the far north end of the beach. Bear right with the road at the little row of fishermen's cottages and continue on to the National Trust car park at Porth Neigwl. Follow the path between the dunes onto the sand then head left towards the south end of the beach.

2 After about fifteen minutes, take a sharp left at the small stream. Walk up the sandy path and over a stile into a field. Head for the next stile in the bottom right- hand corner of the field. Continue and at the third stile go right as directed and follow the right-hand field hedge and low stone wall to the ladder stile ahead. Don't be tempted to cross the attractive little wooden bridge on your right but go left along the grassy track between the rocky outcrop on your right and the wire fence on your left. Continue straight ahead alongside the dramatic lower slopes of the Llanengan escarpment, with its rock, gorse, ivy, and in summer, abundant foxgloves.

3 After a short climb and another few stiles, follow the by now fairly level green path below the lead mine chimney. It is a particularly pleasing chimney, the tapering striations of yellow and red brick giving it the air of a pretty folly rather than a sturdy piece of Industrial Revolution history. The tower of St Engan's church is pretty much straight ahead. Follow the path back to the pub, pick up the key and continue on to the church.

The Church
SH 294270
Access: The church is not open but the key can be obtained from the landlord at the Sun Inn.

The church is one of only two – St Maelrhys is the other – from which Bardsey is visible from the churchyard. There were extremely close ties between the Abby of St Mary's on Bardsey and St Engan's. T. J. Hughes describes St Engan's as the abbey's 'outpost and foothold on the mainland' and suggests that its

Tower with west door

North aisle

bells, its dugout chest, and 'perhaps its rood screen too' came from the abbey after the Dissolution. The screen is, in fact, two screens, both intricately carved, one with a choir loft, spanning between them the width of the church, one screen for each of the two naves. St Engan's doesn't have the luminous charm of St Gwynhoedl's but it is as impressive and equally apt as a final station on the route to Bardsey: St Gwynhoedl's on the northern route, St Engan's on the southern route.

In his book, *Every Pilgrim's Guide to Celtic Britain and Ireland*, Andrew Jones notes that there are two holy wells beyond the western boundary of the churchyard where 'healing was to be received by bathing in one and drinking from the other'.

WALK 6

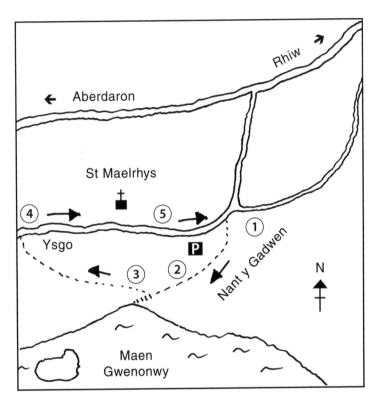

St Maelrhys, Llanfaelrhys

St Maelrhys, Llanfaelrhys

The ghosts of Elsi Thomas and the Keatings
hover in this churchyard above the serene Porth Ysgo

Distance	About a mile and a half
Difficulty	Moderate
Time	Allow an hour and a half
Landscape	Rugged coast and gentle rural lanes
Suggested map	OS Explorer 253 Llŷn Peninsula West
Start/finish	Grid reference: SH 212269
Parking	Park in the pull-in at the bend in the road, just beyond the footpath sign to Porth Ysgo.
Facilities	There are no public toilets or refreshment facilities en route.
Wildflowers	The beautiful spring squill with its delicate blues and, sometimes, mauves dots the grassy cliffs in May.

The Walk

This is a short, gentle walk taking in the lovely valley, Nant y Gadwen, and the compact drama of Porth Ysgo. From this tiny strand, cargoes of manganese from the mines at Rhiw were once loaded onto ships bound for Ellesmere Port. The rusting winches up above lend the beauty of the headland a kind of wistful melancholy. The jetty at Porth Ysgo was last used in 1927.

Directions

1 Go through the kissing gate and follow the obvious enough path down the valley to a second gate and National Trust sign over to your right. The disused mine workings are clearly visible from here.

2 Go through the gate and follow the path until the steps leading down to the beach at Porth Ysgo. The large rock just off-shore is Maen Gwenonwy, named after the brother of King Arthur. Your rather arduous climb back up the steps will be soothed by the cascading of the waterfall, Pistyll y Gaseg, as it tumbles onto the beach below.

3 At the top of the steps return to the path. After a relatively gentle climb up the valley you will come to a little stone bridge beneath which flows the stream that eventually crashes over the cliff at Porth Ysgo. Go right, here, through a signed kissing-gate and along the green path.

4 Go through the ruins of Ysgo Farm and turn right onto the tarmac road. The church is now in view. From here, it could be a shepherd's croft, tucked down low to avoid the westerlies howling in off the Irish Sea, and the swaying bell-rope for raising the alarm rather than calling the faithful to prayer. Enter the churchyard either by the gate in the west wall or over the mounting block in the south wall.

5 To return to your car turn left out of the churchyard. The lay-by is at the bottom of the hill.

The Church
SH 210268
Access: The church is open throughout the year during daylight hours.

St Maelrhys, a classically simple, single-chamber church, stands quite alone in the rough pastures above Porth Ysgo. The Victorian multi-pane windows set in the plain medieval structure make the church look even more like a farm building, though here like an inviting cottage rather than a barn. The huge east window with its clear glass affords dramatic views of Mynydd Rhiw's craggy slopes. The font is fifteenth century but the interior is strikingly Georgian with its box pews on the south side and simple benches on the north. The communion table is early eighteenth century.

West door and bell-cote

St Maelrhys is one of only two churches in Llŷn where Bardsey is visible from the churchyard, the other being St Engan in Llanengan, the last major 'station' for pilgrims making their way to Aberdaron along the southern route.

The churchyard contains the graves of the Keating sisters and their mother, Constance Annie Keating. The sisters – Eileen, Lorna and Mary Honora – share an elegant, horizontal memorial slab lying at the feet of their mother's rough, vertical headstone, as if they huddle still at her protective skirts. Constance's headstone reads, 'Her children shall

Constance Keating's headstone

Box pews and benches

rise up and call her blessed'.

In the 1930s, Constance and her spinster daughters had bought the nearby Jacobean manor, Plas-yn-Rhiw, dedicating their lives to its restoration and to the preservation of this part of coastal Llŷn. They were famously eccentric, admired and mocked in equal measure by the puzzled locals. In *A Place in the Mind*, Gerallt Jones recalls Constance's death, his clergyman father finding 'the old lady's body propped up in a wicker-basket chair by the window, taking the sun'. He goes on, 'When they eventually buried their mother, they did so in the tiny churchyard of Llanfaelrhys, looking out to sea, under a rough boulder. When a farmer tried to build a barn between the grave and the western horizon, they instantly instructed their faithful solicitor to prevent him doing so – it interfered with the old lady's view of the sea'.

The sisters became close friends and benefactors of R. S. Thomas and his wife, Elsi, eventually providing them with the cottage in which they lived after his retirement. Elsi died there. Their only child, Gwydion, lives there still with his family.

'Elsi' Thomas's headstone

Elsi too is buried here at Llanfaelrhys, a couple of paces from the Keatings. All that the tiny memorial stone records of the life of this talented but timid artist rendered effectively invisible by her husband is this:

M. E. Eldridge, 1909–1991

And even in death, it is the husband who gets the last word, even though his ashes are buried miles away at Porthmadog following a second marriage to the improbable Betty Vernon, in Thomas's words, 'a smoking, swearing, drinking, fox-hunting female' whom he married on her eightieth birthday. The not-at-all self-effacing Betty declared to Byron Rogers, Thomas's biographer, 'we had lived in sin, and it was wonderful, then we got respectable'. This little memorial at Llanfaelrhys, beneath the stark name and dates accorded to Elsi, there is this:

Ac yn ei ysbryd
R. S. Thomas
1913–2000

'And in his spirit.' I am not sure what either Elsi or Betty would make of this. Or, indeed, the poet-priest himself, known as 'Ronnie Boy' by the fabulously irreverent Betty.

Walks on the Northern Pilgrim Route

WALK 7

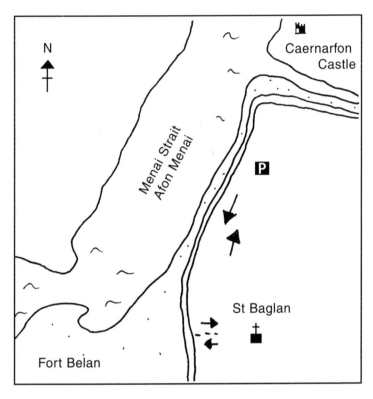

St Baglan, Llanfaglan

St Baglan, Llanfaglan

A mighty castle and a simple church

Landscape	The mudflats, sandbanks and southern salt marsh of Foryd Bay
Distance	About four miles
Difficulty	Easy
Time	Allow two and a half hours
Suggested map	OS Explorer Map 263, Anglesey East
Start/finish	Grid reference: SH 474628
Parking	Park in Caernarfon and make your way past the castle and over the swing-bridge to the road that runs alongside the Strait or drive to this road and park as near to Caernarfon as you can.
Wildflowers	On this walk it is the wildlife on and around the water that dominates rather than the profusion of wildflowers in the fields and hedgerows on the opposite side of the road. Winter, of course, is a particularly good time to observe the comings and goings of the migratory birds feeding on the mudflats and salt-marshes.

The Walk

Despite Snowdonia's massive presence to the east this is a walk whose horizons are close and intimate, even Abermenai Point, Anglesey's southernmost tip, seems to be no more than a skimmed stone's throw across the water. One's eye is drawn not so much to the distant mountains as to the activity on or near the water: the wildlife on the mudflats and sandbanks of Foryd Bay, the modest boats plying the Strait or up on their cradles of

Foryd Bay

stout timber along the banks, the distant figures bent double picking worms for bait from the mud or delicacies for the table, the glimpses of Fort Belan, the only American War of Independence fortification on the eastern side of the Atlantic.

Though Caernarfon is not exactly on the coast, the presence of the sea is pervasive, those harbour smells evoking childhood summers. The lazy drone of single-engine aircraft circling the little Caernarfon airfield also recall long-ago summers. And they call to mind, too, more sombre and more heroic times. In 1941, RAF Llandwrog, a Bomber Command base, was established here. And it was here, in 1942, that Flt Lt GV Graham, the medical officer at the base, formed a 'Mountain Rescue Section', in response to the increasing number of aircraft lost in the mountains of north Wales. Other stations in mountainous areas rapidly took up his idea, and in 1943 the initiative was formally adopted by the RAF, becoming the Mountain Rescue Service.

'The stone-walled llan *laid bare'*

Directions

1 Head south-west alongside the water till you find the church in the field.
2 Head north-east alongside the water back to your car. You will probably be even more conscious of the colossal scale and brutal splendour of Caernarfon Castle after your visit to the self-effacing little church in the field.

The Church

SH 454607

Access: The church is kept locked.

T. J. Hughes describes the church and churchyard of St Baglan's as 'the stone walled *llan* laid bare, a lonely circle in a great green field by the sea'. The church

Yr Eifl from the churchyard

sits at the top of a gentle rise in that field, the trees on the seaward side of the *llan* bent double from the wind, their branches reaching towards the church, like supplicants at a shrine. Sheep huddle in the shade at this western end of the *llan* when the sun is high, and gather on the east side to shelter from the wind when it hurtles in across the Strait. The church is owned by the estimable Friends of Friendless Churches, and for all its isolation, St Baglan's feels anything but abandoned. It is still consecrated and services are still held here on certain occasions.

WALK 8

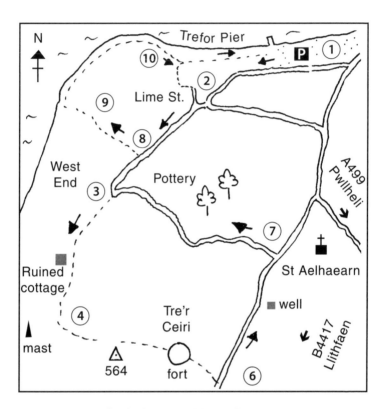

N

Trefor Pier

10

P

1

2

Lime St.

9

West End

8

Pottery

3

7

St Aelhaearn

Ruined cottage

well

4

Tre'r Ceiri

mast

564

fort

6

A499 Pwllheli

B4417 Llithfaen

St Aelhaearn, Llanaelhaearn

St Aelhaearn, Llanaelhaearn

A walk that includes the ancient settlement that has been described as 'the most impressive and dramatic of all British hill forts'

Landscape	Mountain, wooded foothills, coastal headland
Distance	About eight miles
Difficulty	Challenging. Climb of 564 metres to summit of Yr Eifl
Time	Allow a full day to take in the spectacular views from Yr Eifl's highest peak, to enjoy a leisurely picnic, explore the hill fort and the church, and to relax on the unspoilt beach at Trefor before driving home
Suggested map	OS Explorer 254, Llŷn Peninsula East
Start/finish	Grid reference: SH 378474
Parking	In the car-park at Trefor Beach
Facilities	Public toilets in the Trefor Beach car-park during the summer months. Yr Eifl Café in Llanaelhaearn.
Wildflowers	Gorse and heather on the mountainsides and the extraordinary bog-cotton in the marshy areas on the approach to both the highest peak on Yr Eifl and the easternmost peak, site of the Tre'r Ceiri hill fort. Thrift is in abundance on the grassy Morfa headland.

The Walk

From Trefor you climb to the Bronze Age cairn on the highest of Yr Eifl's three peaks before making your way to the dramatic and extraordinarily well-preserved Iron Age fort, Tre'r Ceiri (*tre*: town/settlement; *ceiri*: giants), on the easternmost peak. After visiting the church in the village of Llanaelhaearn you take the

Yr Eifl, Trei'r Ceiri beyond

winding lane down past the ancient woodlands of the medieval township of Elernion and arrive back at the coast at the austere 'West End'. From here you make your way back to Trefor over the National Trust headland at Morfa, where the sea booms in the caves beneath, the sheep nibble and jostle at the very edge of the cliffs, and the guillemots gather on jagged Ynys Fawr, shiny and sleek, preparing to dive. On Trefor Beach, at the foot of majestic Gyrn Ddu, there may be perhaps half a dozen boats at anchor in the lee of the granite harbour wall, and even on a hot summer's day, no more than a handful of children playing on the sand, paddling in the shallows, or crab fishing off the harbour steps.

The village of Llanaelhaearn lies below the eastern slopes of Yr Eifl and is roughly 500 feet above sea level, 1,000 feet closer to the sea than the summit but exposed, nevertheless, to the merciless northerlies blowing down the mountain. Such shelter as there is is afforded by the yew trees to the north and west of the churchyard.

Directions

1 From the car park head past the pier, through the wooden gate and along the path heading west. Shortly after the wooden bridge over the stream follow the lane as it curves to the left. Continue to the end of the lane and turn left at the bus depot.

2 Turn right before the bridge onto Lime Street, walking to the bridge at the far end where you again turn right. This marks the start of the long ascent of the mountain. Follow the road as it climbs, ignoring footpath signs to the right and to the left.

3 After about half a mile, and where the road makes a sharp bend to the left, continue straight ahead onto the green lane marked with a footpath sign. From here the old Yr Eifl quarry workings have the air of some Moorish alcazar, particularly when the sky beyond it is as intensely blue as it is surprisingly often at this western edge of Wales. Continue climbing to the ruined cottage, where you may well want to draw breath and to enjoy the now dizzyingly panoramic views out over Caernarfon Bay. Continue climbing until the fence that has been on your right for some while veers off towards the quarry and the radio mast. Follow the fence until you come upon a grassy path that will take you onto a broad, rocky road. Turn left.

4 At the telegraph pole immediately opposite the gate onto the service track up to the radio mast, turn left onto the grassy track and begin the climb up to the shale and rock-fall. Continue straight up the wide path then onto a little narrow path off to the right through the heather. Take the left fork at the shale. This well-defined path continues on and up through the shale, cleverly-distributed yellow shingle both marking the route and aiding grip. Head towards a little pile of yellow stone in amongst the rocks where the path continues. Scramble up the cairn to the trig point, the highest point on the peninsula. Notice, too, the circular stone structure next to the trig point. Was this a lookout hut to give

the fort at Trei'r Ceiri ample warning of attacks from the sea to the west? Now to the west you can see the old quarrymen's cottages below the wooded slopes of Nant Gwrtheyrn, the odd lobster fisherman bobbing about out to sea beyond Porth y Nant, and further down, the elegant curve of Nefyn and the even more graceful sweep of Porthdinllaen. Looking south and east, the outlines of the Iron Age fort are clear enough.

5 Climb down the cairn on the south side and onto the path and at the fork take the left-hand path as it descends towards the hill fort. The path remains pretty clear, if intermittent, until the land levels out at a marshy, reedy area of ground. Go straight across here, still heading towards the fort. The path becomes more defined again. Head for the gap in the wall and the information board nearby. Go through the gap in the outer rampart, take the right-hand path and climb to the gate into the inner rampart. Once inside, head left for the longest tour of the fort. Maybe a hundred metres or so further on you come to another and more dramatic gate into the ramparts, this one with a huge capstone still in place. Continue round, remaining close to the inner rampart, noting those single, double, and multiple chamber huts. Leave the fort at the obvious exit and head down towards the steps. Go left at the waymark and descend on the now paved version of the path. Go over the ladder stile, down through the gate, keeping the wall on your left-hand side.

6 Go through the last gate and out onto the road, turning left towards Llanaelhaearn. Most of this section can be walked on the attractive grassy bank on the opposite side of the road. Just before the village, where the road flattens out, the dreary little garage or outhouse on your right turns out to be St Aelhaearn's well, sadly no longer accessible since it was roofed in the 1920s. Once in the village, take the first right down to the church.

7 From the church return to the B4177, and almost immediately cross over to the small road straight ahead. Remain on this road for the next mile and a half or so as it climbs before beginning the long descent to the sea. Continue on down into the increasingly wooded lower slopes past the pottery and eventually past the point at which you began the ascent up the green lane. Not far from here you climb the stone steps up to the gate at the footpath sign on the left.

8 Go straight across this field to the next gate. Go down to the bottom left-hand corner of the field and the kissing-gate out onto the road. Turn left onto this road, passing underneath the bridge which used to carry not railway lines but the tram tracks for the trucks heading for the landing stage on Trefor beach carrying granite from the quarry. A neighbour of mine whose father was a quarryman used to ride these trucks after school, hurtling down the tracks to the beach.

9 At the cottages follow the footpath sign to the left, then go right at the National Trust sign, Nant Bach. Continue along the path towards the ocean and go through the field gate, heading still closer to the sea. Aim for the bottom left-corner of the field and another field gate. Turn right along the green path then, shortly after the whitewashed cottages, go left down towards the sea. At the point where the path divides three ways, go right, keeping the sea on your left as you climb to the wooden kissing-gate. You are now on the Morfa headland. Keep straight ahead, choosing how close you wish to go to the cliff edge. The paths more or less midway between the fence and the sea are probably the best bet, avoiding not only the cliff edge but the various gullies that could be difficult to cross or laborious to circumvent.

10 When you see Trefor Pier keep straight ahead, descend to the kissing-gate and make your way to the car-park.

Yr Eifl, Trefor pier in the distance

North wall

The Church
SH 387448
Access: The church is kept locked.

Little is known of St Aelhaearn. He is said to have been a follower of Beuno, and probably founded his community here in the early seventh century. Striking evidence of a much earlier Christian presence on this site can be found in the memorial stone now attached to the wall of the north transept inside the church. This rough stone, unearthed in the middle of the nineteenth century in a nearby field – Gardd Sant (*gardd*: garden; *sant*: saint) – is reckoned to be from the late fourth or early fifth century. Its Latin inscription reads, '*Aliortus Elmetiaco hic iacet*', ('Here lies Aliortus, a man from Elmet'). Elmet, roughly the area now known as West Yorkshire, was an ancient British Kingdom whose inhabitants spoke a form of early Welsh. Aliortus was clearly an important figure, a leader perhaps in one of the periodic waves of migration from the Old North (southern Scotland and northern Britain) to north Wales during the fifth century. Aelhaearn himself, a follower of Beuno, is likely to have founded his *llan* here at least 100 years after the man from Elmet was laid to rest.

There are two other ancient inscribed stones within the *llan*: another fifth-century memorial stone to one Melitus and a cross-incised stone from the seventh to ninth centuries. The Melitus stone stands alone near the path to the west door, the cross-incised stone is set into the retaining wall within the churchyard near the west porch.

The present church, like so many of lŷn's churches, is the result of successive waves of building, restoration and embellishment between the twelfth and the seventeenth centuries. The most recent renovation was in 2009. In the south transept there is a memorial to Catherine, eldest daughter of Richard Glyn of Elernion, who died in 1702. You will pass above the atmospheric Elernion along the lower, wooded section of the

Rood screen

Aliortus Stone

Melitus Stone

walk from the church back to the sea.

The headstones in the churchyard – many of them corralled within rusting railings – line the avenue leading to the gate in the north boundary wall, beyond which is only sea, mountains and sky. These lopsided memorials seem all the more poignant against the pitiless beauty of this backdrop.

North side of the llan

WALK 9

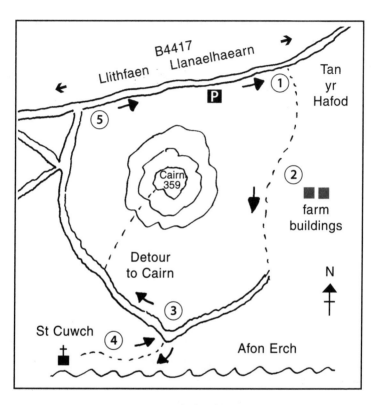

St Cuwch, Carnguwch

St Cuwch, Carnguwch

*The most abandoned
and perhaps the most affecting of all the churches*

Landscape	Ancient farmland at the foot of the mountain
Distance	About five miles but more if you decide to climb to the perfect Bronze Age cairn at the summit of Mynydd Carnguwch.
Difficulty	Moderate
Time	Allow about three hours
Suggested map	OS Explorer 253, Llŷn Peninsula West
Start/finish	Grid reference: SH 372437
Parking	Pull in at the lay-by at this grid reference on the B4177 between Llanaelhaearn and Llithfaen.
Facilities	There are no public toilets or refreshment facilities en route
Wildflowers	Meadow buttercups light up the rough pasture from May to August and the higher slopes of Mynydd Carnguwch are rich with the brilliant bell heather. In late summer the ancient, walled track to the church is heavy with blackberries and orange plumes of montbretia shoot from the hedge like tongues of fire.

The Walk

The church is reachable only on foot: from the north, down a green lane between ancient walls; and from the south, up a farm lane from the tiny hamlet of Llwyndyrys. This walk takes the northern route.

Approaching the church across the ragged field at the end of the green lane, one is unprepared for the startling beauty of the south side of the *llan*. Just beyond the south wall the rough ground drops suddenly and steeply to a wooded valley, where Afon Erch winds unhurriedly below the trees on the opposite slope. Cattle amble across a grassy bridge, perilously close to its unprotected sides. It is not hard to imagine the feelings of whichever follower of Beuno it was that came upon this spot and built his hut here. Looking down at this bright ribbon of water, these wooded slopes, this lush pasture, he must surely have found his Eden.

Directions

1 From the lay-by walk back down the hill towards Llanaelhaearn. In a couple of hundred metres or so turn right onto the track at Tan yr Hafod farm.

2 Just before the farm buildings turn right onto the generous grassy track. There are wonderful views of Cardigan Bay ahead. Behind you, to the north, you can catch glimpses of Caernarfon Bay in the dramatic V between Gyrn Ddu and Yr Eifl. After a few hundred metres go through the field gate and onto the great green trackway, passing ancient stunted trees and the ruins of a cottage. Go through another (permanently open) field gate, then through an enormously wide field gate, turning right onto the tarmac lane. You are now heading south-west, and as the lane rises, Llanbedrog headland and Tudwal's Islands come into view.

3 At a distinct dip in the lane, a few hundred metres further on, you will see two gates on your left. Go over the first of these gates and continue down the green lane between the dense hedges of gorse and brambles, heavy with fruit in late summer. You may notice over to your right a low, modest roof in amongst the trees, like the plain cottage of a recluse. This is the roof of St Beuno's church. Climb the next gate and continue along the green lane, now flanked by evocative old stone walls. At the next field gate (with its ingenious

counter-weight) cross the often boggy field to the church.

4   Return up the green lane and turn left on reaching the tarmac road. (If you want to see the perfect Bronze Age cairn at the summit of Mynydd Carnguwch take the track off to your right about 100 metres or so before the white cottage on your left. After this detour you can return to the road a little higher up, just beyond the white cottage).

5   Continue until the crossroads where you turn right onto the narrow lane that will take you back to the B4177. Turn right. The lay-by is a five minute walk from here.

The Church
SH 374418
Access: The church is kept permanently locked. It doesn't belong any more to the diocese and has not been adopted by the Friends of Friendless Churches. I have not been able to identify a key holder.

In his *A Description of Caernarvonshire*, from 1811, Edmund Hyde Hall declares that it is 'in a condition utterly disgraceful to a Christian community'. Only forty years later, in *A Topographical Dictionary of Wales*, Samuel Lewis calls it 'a small, neat edifice'. T. J. Hughes describes it as:

the most human and restoring of places, its long views beautiful and lonely, and its churchyard more filled with original poetry, and with the sense of the worth of the people who lie there, than any comparable other.

All three writers capture something of the particular quality of this humble, isolated building. But it is hard not to be shocked by its condition, its abandoned, even desolate air. Like its namesake at Pistyll it, too, is encircled by mountains, and sits within its graciously curving *llan*, close to running water and woodland. But there is no strewing of rushes and sweet-

Approaching this remote church

Church and llan

smelling herbs here. There is no congregation, and so far as I have been able to ascertain, no-one to befriend this most friendless of churches. Its windows are boarded like a house awaiting demolition. And yet there is a sense of life here in this overgrown churchyard. The lives of long-gone congregations are often memorialised in *englynion*. T. J. Hughes quotes one such inscription, on the memorial to Evan Jones of Caernarfon, describing it as 'a perfect *englyn*':

Fy ngfeullion Wuwlon Wedd na Wulwch
Pan Weloch fy anedd
Chwi yn fud or bud ir bedd
Attaf dowch yn y diwedd

> [My friends, with your downcast faces,
> Don't cry when you see my home.
> Silently, from the world to the grave,
> You will come to join me in the end.]

Perhaps, as T. J. Hughes suggests, this church, for all its remoteness, was 'linked by the chain of pilgrimage' to the other churches on the northern route to Bardsey from the mother church at Clynnog Fawr. Perhaps those great caravans of people and animals did indeed tramp from Llanaelhaearn down below Mynydd Carnguwch before climbing up again to Llithfaen and on to Pistyll. But it doesn't feel like that. Its origins seem to lie in the quest for solitariness, its history to be the uneventful history of generations of isolated families seeking solace and community. The novelty of strangers, the tumult of pilgrimage, seem to have no place here. It is both forlorn and uplifting, the most desolate and the most affecting of all the churches.

There is some dispute as to the dedication of this church, some authorities believing it to be dedicated to St Beuno, others to the obscure St Cuwch. St Cuwch's very obscurity seems to me to suit this lost church perfectly.

WALK 10

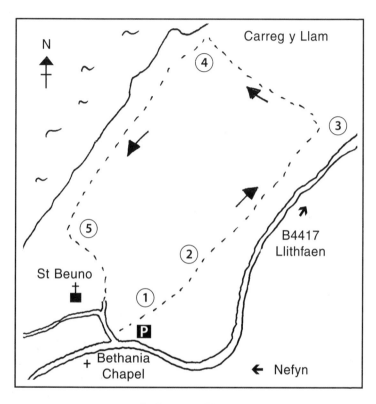

St Beuno, Pistyll

WALK 10
St Beuno, Pistyll

A medieval hospice church where
medicinal herbs still grow wild on the surrounding hills

Landscape	Coastal hills with panoramic views of the Cambrian Coast
Distance	About three miles or five if you continue on to the medieval cross-incised stone on the road to Nefyn
Difficulty	Moderate
Time	Allow two to three hours
Suggested map	OS Explorer 253, Llŷn Peninsula West
Start/finish	Grid reference: SH 329422
Parking	National Trust car-park
Facilities	There are no public toilets or refreshment facilities en route
Wildflowers	Spectacular gorse on the slopes, and down below the church, alongside the fast-running brook, ash, alder, willow, blackthorn and hawthorn have colonised the banks. Lady's smock and St John's wort are among the more uncommon wildflowers that can be seen on this walk.

The Walk

At the highest point in the walk you will be looking down at Porth y Nant. This stretch of pebble beach is at the foot of the vertiginous Nant Gwrtheyrn, where a quarrying community lived until the industry ceased in the mid-1950s. There are remains of jetties and of winding gear on the beach still. The village, abandoned for over twenty years, was restored by a group of local business-people in the 1970s and is now a residential language and cultural centre.

Legend has it that Nant Gwrtheyrn is where the fifth century British warlord, Vortigern (or Gwrtheyrn, St Madrun's grandfather) ended up when the Saxon mercenaries he had employed turned on him, forcing him to flee further and further into the west. The valley has a mournful and inspiring air, a kind of terrible beauty.

Shortly beyond this high point you begin the descent towards the sea and the church. There are clear views of the seductive Porthdinllaen throughout the descent. Ponder, as you scramble down, how this view might have looked had a certain Parliamentary vote in 1837 had a different outcome. The vote was to decide whether Porthdinllaen or Holyhead should become the main port for the Irish Sea crossing to Dublin. Holyhead won by just one vote, miraculously leaving the serene Porthdinllaen just as you see it now.

Directions

1   Go through the wooden gate at the right hand corner of the car park and make for the obvious green path that sweeps away to the left as it climbs up through the gorse. Before you begin the climb you may be tempted by the sign, 'Ffynnon Sanctaid', to look at the promised holy well. Unhappily, all that is now visible are the six slabs covering the well opening.

2   The path climbs steadily between little stone-and-earth banks, past farm buildings on your right and, eventually, out onto an open field. Keep to the right hand side of the field and go through another, permanently open field gate. Continue upwards through two more gates, following the line of telegraph poles. Notice the raised earthworks of hut circle remains.

3   At the crest of the hill make for the farm buildings that you will now see at the lower left hand end of the field. Head towards the gate in the wall to the right of the farm. Go through the gate and continue along the well-maintained green lane between impressive *clawdd* banks. Go through

the next kissing gate then through the unusual and charming gated stile on the top of the bank. Turn right and go through the metal field gate by the caravan on your left. Go alongside the caravan and through a wooden kissing gate. Make your way to the stile in the top left hand corner of the field. Continue along the little green lane and turn left onto the rough, stony track heading downhill. Continue past the white house with its battalions of exotic, strutting cockerels and on through the field gate at the bungalow, 'Carreg y Llam'. The path continues over a cattle grid beneath which the stream continues its headlong rush to the sea. Continue onto what was probably the Carreg y Llam quarry's service road, still edged with huge boulders. Take the left fork at the start of the climb up the hill (and the right fork for a detour to the long disused quarry).

4 Head for the bench, more or less straight ahead, perched improbably but invitingly on the seaward edge of this sweep of land. There are no more challenging ascents on this walk and the bench is likely to be welcome. You are now on the edge of the seabird sanctuary, Carreg y Llam. The view, from here, down to Porth y Nant, is awe-inspiring. Shortly beyond the bench go through a kissing gate and continue up the gentle climb, keeping to the right. The green path flattens out then begins the exceptionally lovely descent towards the sea and the church. Continue down the fairly obvious tracks that often run alongside the remains of old buildings, perhaps ruined cottages from the heyday of quarrying in the 1870s. As the land flattens out, head towards the wooden field gate straight ahead.

5 Take the lower path here through the kissing gate and along the raised green causeway where the roof of St Beuno's will begin to come into view. Go through the next kissing gate and walk alongside the wall of the *llan* until the gate into the churchyard. To return to the car park continue down the path and turn left onto the lane. To walk to the cross-incised

stone, turn right instead onto the lane and make for the gaunt and melancholy ruins of the old hotel.

The incised stone is not obvious (and in the height of summer effectively invisible) but worth tracking down. Nothing like the monumental boulder at Clynnog Fawr, this is a modest stone that now serves a practical purpose at the base of a rough but sturdy boundary wall. This functionality doesn't lessen one's sense of its original use as a marker but also a ritual object. Grateful to have got this far, the pilgrims would trace the incised sign of the cross with their fingers and pray for the strength and courage to continue.

The walk back along the main road has its own interests, not least the austere but pleasing Calvinistic Methodist Capel Bethania and its striking memorial to the local man and hero, the minister Thomas Williams, or 'Tom Nefyn', as he is widely known. Following his experiences in the First World War he became an ardent pacifist, but it was as a social reformer that he fell out with the Presbyterian authorities in the aftermath of the General Strike. After a period in a spiritual wilderness he returned to the Nefyn area in the 1940s, where his reputation as an electrifying preacher drew huge crowds to his meetings at roadsides, street corners and fairgrounds, and even, apparently, on the clifftops at Nefyn. The three-quarter profile bas-relief shows a fierce but handsome face, now dramatically weathered by those salty winds. The inscription translates roughly as:

He was a candle shedding light and burning down
The reverend
Tom Nefyn Williams
1895-1958
A native of Pistyll
Quarryman
Benefactor
Evangelist

It has to be said that Tom Nefyn, up here in the teeth of the wind, has at least as powerful a presence as that 'tall man' snug in the wooded hollow of St Beuno's below.

Directions to cross-incised stone SH 319418

1 Walk alongside the ruinous hotel to the very attractive wooden kissing-gate. Cross the field to the next stile. The village of Pistyll is up above you on the left, the end wall of the chapel facing due north, fearless in its righteousness, facing down those furious winds off the sea.

2 At the next kissing-gate cross the little tarmac track to the gate and go into the field. Go more or less straight ahead to the gap in the low stone wall and onto the path beyond. Go right along this path until the metal kissing-gate. At this point head down on the lower path to the right of the fence. The graceful arc of Porthdinllaen is now in full view.

South wall

East wall

North wall of the llan

3   Go through the next gate, cross the little wooden bridge over the brook, and up the stone steps. Turn sharp left, climb the field to the top left-hand corner then follow the *clawdd* bank boundary and head for the ruined cottage. Climb the stile just beyond the cottage and head across the field towards the gate in the bottom left-hand corner. Follow the little path up to the main road. Turn right onto the road and walk the couple of hundred metres or so to the ancient stone, now embedded in the field boundary wall on your left.

4   To return to your car head back along the B4417 through Pistyll. The sea is vast on your left, the tallest peak of Yr Eifl is straight ahead, and to your right is the modest but shapely Moel Tŷ-gwyn.

The Church
SH 328423
Access: The church is open throughout the year during daylight hours.

Originally founded in the sixth century by St Beuno, this hospice church is a near-perfect example of an early Celtic foundation, with its circular churchyard in a sheltered hollow, the wooded grove nearby, the stream running alongside, the sea and the mountains within view. The twelfth-century building itself, with its 'leper's window' in the north wall, the monastic fishpond just beyond the churchyard wall, the adjacent field-names – 'Cae Hospis', for example – speak eloquently of its medieval past and its importance during the age of pilgrimage, as do the medicinal herbs – fennel, camomile, rosemary – still growing vigorously on the hillsides, and the fruit bushes and hop vines in the remains of the ash grove. The floor of the church is strewn with rushes and herbs three times a year: at Christmas, Easter and at Lammas, on the first day of August, when bread baked with 'the first fruits of the harvest' is brought to the church. This strewing of the floor is a practice of relatively recent origin but one that makes a powerful connection with the medieval church on this spot.

Some believe that the 'the tall man' interred beneath the altar in this little single-chamber church is the mortal remains of the miracle-worker and missionary St Beuno, the most celebrated of all the northern Welsh saints.

The churchyard rises sharply from its sheltered, western boundary to the exposed east wall battered by the fierce winds blowing off Caernarfon Bay. Just in the lee of this wall is the grave of Rupert Davies, fondly remembered as Maigret in the TV series. One imagines him cupping that struck match, shielding it from the north winds whipping off the sea. The last line of the epitaph on his headstone is apt and moving:

> Remembered with affection by thousands
> who had never met him.

Surely, a saint would be happy with such an epitaph. Even 'the tall man' buried in the body of the church, whoever he may be.

WALK 11

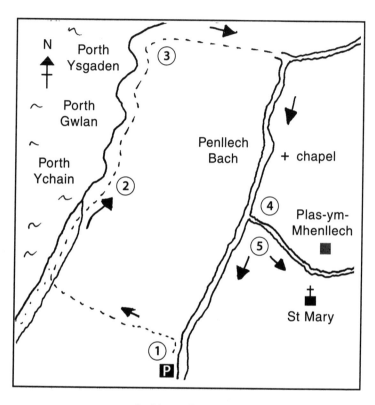

St Mary, Penllech

St Mary, Penllech

The starkly beautiful church at Plas ym Mhenllech Farm

Landscape	Exposed cliff-top paths and sheltered rural lanes
Distance	About five miles
Difficulty	Easy
Time	Allow three hours
Suggested map	OS Explorer 253, Llŷn Peninsula West
Start/finish	Grid reference: SH 207343
Parking	In the Traeth Penllech car-park
Facilities	There are no public toilets or refreshment facilities en route
Wildflowers	Abundant sea pinks in summer along the cliff-top paths. The hedgerows along the lanes are profuse with flowers throughout the spring and summer, from the demure primrose in early spring to the showy red campion in midsummer to the positively flamboyant rosebay willowherb, or fireweed, in late summer and early autumn.

The Walk

Even as you walk the quiet, high-hedged lanes, out of sight of the coast, it is the sea that dominates, defining not only the western horizon but the limits of the mind's eye. It is from this sea that the raiders and the saints emerged, bringing the sword or the Word, scrambling ashore at the little, sheltered coves that you visit on this walk: Porth Ychain, Porth Gwylan, and Porth Ysgaden.

The first half of the walk takes you along the cliff-top paths from the silvery strand at Traeth Penllech to craggy Porth

Ysgaden, with its herring fishing history, its old limestone kiln, and mysterious ruin up on the headland. On the second half of the walk you follow the sheltered lanes to the church at Plas ym Mhenllech before dropping down to the bridge, Pont-yr-Afon, where the stream that runs round the *llan* at Llangwnnadl heads across the fields before cascading onto the beach at Traeth Penllech.

Directions

1   From the car-park walk onto the lane and turn immediately left onto the footpath. Go through the gate and into the open field. Follow the obvious path towards the sea, noting the tumbling waterfall as you approach the beach. Turn right and walk along the beach after a few minutes climbing up onto the cliff path at the stile.

2   Walk alongside the large fenced fields to your right. Sheep graze both within these enclosed fields and out on the paths and, often, down on the cliff edges. Sometimes they are to be seen ambling and munching within inches of the unperturbed horses that occasionally grace these fields. Continue on, past Porth Ychain and Porth Gwlan, until the atmospheric Porth Ysgaden with its distinctive, stony beach and the mysterious ruin on the headland above.

3   At the wooden kissing-gate at Porth Ysgaden head right onto the stony track and follow it to the junction with the lane. Turn right and continue as this little road bisects the ancient-looking farm, Tyddyn Isaf, where geese and ducks potter busily on the road. Continue along the lane towards Penllech, passing the very appealing chapel at Penllech Bach, the anchor motifs on the façade testimony to the central place of the sea in the lives of this community.

4   About half a mile or so further on turn left onto the lane immediately opposite a blue Cycle Route sign and walk the short distance to the magnificent farm, Plas ym Mhenllech. The church will be found on the right.

The east wall

5   To return go back down the lane from the church and turn left onto the road at the T junction. The car park is about a mile away.

The Church
SH 220344
Access: The church is open throughout the year during daylight hours.

Talking to an Aberdaron man about my walks to local churches he asked if I'd visited Plas ym Mhenllech. He looked puzzled, at first, when I asked him if he meant St Mary at Penllech. He, along with other natives of the area, knew the church well but knew it by the name of the farm to which it is adjacent. This could not be more appropriate. This is yet another simple, single-chamber church in that vernacular farmyard style typical of the region. The twist here is that St Mary's is as much a part

The sea beyond the churchyard

Looking towards the altar

of Plas ym Mhenllech as the farmhouse and the barns, the whole complex patrolled by the friendly but watchful Border Collie. This is the rural church incarnate: a muddy, workaday place where there must surely be a powerful connection between the natural and the ritual seasons and between the metaphorical and the literal language of lambs and shepherds and fishermen.

The church is about a mile as the crow flies from the great expanse of the Irish Sea. It is hard to resist the impression that the headstones in the churchyard are lined up like deck chairs, their occupants eternally contemplating the distant swell. Very near the door there is an impressive monumental slab from the early nineteenth century. It is difficult to read who is commemorated here but very easy indeed to read the beautifully-wrought inscription running along the bottom of the slab:

This tomb is not to be openned. (*sic*)

There are many moving memorials here in this windswept place, not least the small but elegant slate markers that carry no names or dates or consoling texts but initials only, one below the other, exactly like the scrawls of anonymous lovers on a wall or a rock or a tree.

The church, which is always open, has recently been renovated by the Friends of Friendless Churches with the financial assistance of CADW. The bulk of the structure dates from the 1840 restoration, as signified by the date carved above the door, although it is believed that sections of the chancel and the bowl of the font are medieval. The interior is nevertheless particularly striking and evocative of a much later era. The box pews, the pulpit with its elaborate sounding-board, the sconces, and the simple windows all conjure an unmistakeably Georgian world.

In his description of Penllech, Samuel Lewis refers to the good quality of the local arable and pasture land and continues:

Sounding board above pulpit

Bier propped against wall

The inhabitants are principally employed in agricultural pursuits, except during the season of the herring-fishery, which is carried on to a considerable extent. Of the great quantity of herrings taken on this coast, part is salted and sent coastwise for the supply of distant markets.

His pithy comment on the church itself is telling, casting yet another light on the intimate link between the spiritual and the all too material life of this rural church:

The church, dedicated to St Mary, is not distinguished for any architectural detail of importance. Two benefactions in money, amounting to £12.10s, are lost to the poor, having been lent to a farmer who became insolvent some time since.

WALK 12

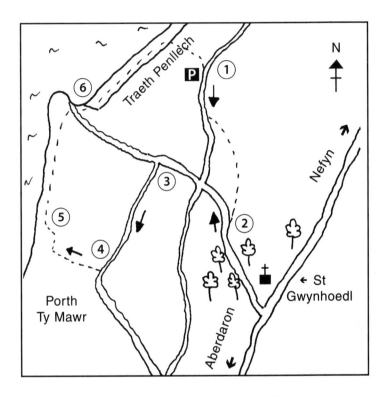

St Gwynhoedl, Llangwnnadl

108

WALK 12
St Gwynhoedl, Llangwnnadl

The last of the hospice churches
on the northern route to Bardsey

Landscape	Rural lanes and cliff-top paths
Distance	About four miles
Difficulty	Moderate
Time	Allow three hours
Suggested map	OS Explorer Map 253, Llŷn Peninsula West
Start/finish	Grid reference: SH 207343
Parking	Park in the Traeth Penllech car-park
Facilities	There are no public toilets or refreshment facilities en route
Wildflowers	There are three distinct terrains on this walk: the wooded dell where the *llan* sits, the hedgerows and fields alongside the lanes to Porth Ty Mawr, and the cliff paths back to Traeth Penllech. Each section is distinguished by its own particular flora – early bluebells and celandines in the wooded area of the church, cranesbill and campion in the hedgerows, red valerian, tormentil and lady's bedstraw on the rocky inlets and outcrops of the coast.

The Walk

Heading north-east along the cliff-top paths is an unusual though uniquely rewarding way of walking the northern coast. You may miss the romance and mystery of walking to the point where the peninsula slips inexorably into the sea but you will not be dazzled by the sun. Instead the sun will be at your back, bringing clarity and radiance to the vistas of ocean, rolling plain and distant mountains.

Directions

1 From the car park walk back to the main road and turn right. After about a quarter of a mile follow the footpath sign to your left. Head diagonally across the field to your right to the marked stile and bridge over the brook. Continue straight ahead following the well-marked path to the Llangwnnadl Community Hall. Turn left onto the road. The church is a hundred metres or so from here.

2 After visiting the church turn right onto the road and, in a hundred metres or so, climb the stile on your left onto the 'Pilgrim's Way' footpath.

3 Go to the top right hand corner of the field and over the bridge on the recently – and expertly – renovated footpath. Continue to the top left-hand corner of the next field, keep left along the path and follow the yellow arrow around the barn, emerging through the farm gate onto the lane. Turn right and then right again at the main road. Cross the marked stile on the left a couple of hundred metres along the road. Follow the attractive path along the top of the *clawdd* bank, across another field, through the gate, around the cottage and up the steps onto the next – short – stretch of bank-top path. Descend to the track, head right to the lane then turn left. A few hundred metres or so along the lane you come to the footpath sign marked. 'Porth Tŷ Mawr'.

4 Walk the stony track until it runs out at ruined farm buildings and a big metal field gate. At this gate go immediately right and cross the field to the bottom left hand corner. At the stile head left. Go straight ahead down the lovely, cropped green path. At the 'junction' continue straight ahead. At the yellow arrow go left up onto the field where you will soon reach a stile on your right. Cross the stile and continue alongside the lively little stream and between the gorse banks until reaching the large signpost up abosve the cliff edge.

5 Go right here and follow the easy route alongside the large,

fenced fields on your right and the great expanse of Caernarfon Bay to your left. Descend the steps to the evocative Porth Golman before climbing up again and walking to Traeth Penllech. If the tide is far enough out, descend to the beach at the first opportunity. If not, take the second path down to the beach.

6 Continue along the silvery-white sands of this most perfect of beaches and climb up the rough path to the gate with the red lifebelt alongside. Go through the gate and where the path flattens out head to the right of the field to see the waterfalls that tumble down to the beach. Follow the river, past the handful of cows usually grazing alongside it at its widest point, and then walk the little wooded path back to the road and the car park.

The Church
SH 209333
Access: The church is open throughout the year during daylight hours.

For me the loveliest of all the churches, St Gwynhoedl's is both the embodiment of the simple Celtic church and a Tudor cathedral in miniature. It sits within its heavily wooded hollow, the stream babbling busily below the south wall of the *llan*, like so many of the churches in Llŷn. Unlike those churches, however, St Gwynhoedl's original twelfth-century single chamber structure was tripled in size, in the 1520s, by the addition of north and south aisles of equal size.

St Gwynhoedl's was the last major resting place for pilgrims following the northern route to Bardsey, and as Gwynhoedl himself is believed to be buried here, it was a significant shrine in its own right. No doubt pilgrim offerings, as with St Beuno's at Clynnog Fawr, helped fund the ambitious Tudor building programme. And in common with Clynnog Fawr it was subject to the historic irony that the practice of pilgrimage was soon to

Ty Dduw (the house of God)

be wiped out by the Reformation's cultural revolution. Quite unlike the vast collegiate church dominating little Clynnog Fawr, however, St Gwynhoedl's is absolutely at one with its setting. Nothing here is jarring or disproportionate or overweening. St Gwynhoedl's sits within its tranquil *llan* with exactly the same kind of modest reserve as its far simpler cousins elsewhere. Which is why entering this elegant space, flooded with light from the generous Perpendicular windows, comes as such a delightful shock.

The church provided a shock of a quite different order for Dr Johnson and Mrs Thrale on their tour of north Wales in 1774. In his diary entry for August 24 Johnson says this of Llangwnnadl and Tudweiliog:

The churches are mean and neglected to a degree scarcely imaginable. They have no pavement, and the earth is full of holes, the seats are rude benches. The altars have no rails;

112

Harvest time

one of them has a breach in the roof. On the desk I think of each lay a Folio Welsh Bible of the black letter, which the Curate cannot easily read.

Mrs Thrale, in her diary entry for the same day, writes that the churches 'shock me with their poverty and misery'. She notes, too, a conversation with the housekeeper of Mr Griffiths in Cefnamlwch who was asked:

> Who was the Parson of the Parish, and where he lived. What! says she, do you mean Jack Roberts? You are come at a bad time to see Jack Roberts, for he has just got a black eye fighting for a girl with an excise man.

The approach to the church is particularly delightful; not least the little church gate with its Celtic cross and – in black lettering on a white ground – the inscription Tŷ Dduw or 'House of God'. The information leaflet available inside the church tells us this gate was 'made and gifted by the late Mr William Jones, village blacksmith at Aberdaron, who is buried in the churchyard'. Also in the churchyard is the grave of 'Griffith Griffiths, Gent', of Methlem, who lived under nine sovereigns, all of whom are listed, from Oliver Cromwell to George II.

JOURNEY'S END

WALK 13

St Hywyn

St Hywyn, Aberdaron

116

St Hywyn, Aberdaron

*An inspiring walk dominated by Bardsey
even when it's not visible*

Landscape	Coastal headland at the very tip of the peninsula
Distance	About six miles
Difficulty	Moderate
Time	Allow four hours
Suggested map	OS Explorer 253, Llŷn Peninsula West
Start/finish	Grid reference: SH 172264
Parking	In the National Trust car-park in the centre of the village
Facilities	Public toilets in the car-park. Two cafes in the village, including the medieval Y Gegin Fawr, and two pubs, Y Llong and Tŷ Newydd
Wildflowers	The *clawdd* banks of Uwchmynydd's medieval patchwork of fields are brilliant with flowers from April to September and the cliffs themselves are alive with colour, from the blue spring squill in May to the nodding pink of thrift later in the summer. The headland of Braich y Pwll, according to the National Trust, is the only known location on the British mainland for spotted rockrose. The area, like the island two miles across the Sound, is also home to rare lichens, liverworts and mosses.

The Walk

The walk is celebrated for its natural beauty but also for its significance in the story of early Christianity and medieval pilgrimage. The footprint of the medieval world is everywhere: the ghostly outline in the grass of St Mary's Church at Braich-y-Pwll; the sturdy, fourteenth-century café in Aberdaron, Y Gegin Fawr (*cegin*: kitchen; *mawr*: big), still providing sustenance for visitors; and tiny Porth Meudwy, from where expectant passengers are still ferried across the two miles of treacherous tidal-race to Bardsey. Bardsey is not visible from Aberdaron or, indeed, even from Porth Meudwy. It rears suddenly into view for the first time at Pen-y-Cil, its inscrutable magnetism at its most powerful at this point, with its back to you, that blank wall of cliffs and caves revealing nothing.

On this walk, too, the faint voices of those trusting medieval pilgrims are joined by the astringent, modern voice of the recent vicar of Aberdaron, R. S. Thomas, who strode this headland, clambered over these rocks, watching and waiting for those birds that were his passion, scornful of the petitions of a simpler faith, and:

> Prayers like gravel
> Flung at the sky's
> Window, hoping to attract
> The loved one's
> Attention.

But the sense of a still-present medieval world extends beyond the sacred and may perhaps be even more strongly present in the earthy realities of the fields and the farms. From the top of Mynydd Mawr, with its views of Bardsey to the south-west, Caernarfon Bay and Anglesey to the north, Snowdonia to the east, and the expanse of Cardigan Bay to the south-east, it may be not so much these distant, spectacular views that claim your attention as the pattern of the fields of Uwchmynydd spread out at your feet: a brilliant medieval patchwork, each square with its *clawdd* bank stitching of stone and bramble and wild flowers.

You will walk the top of one of these banks on the return to Aberdaron.

Shortly after, you will walk past the imposing *Cwrt*, now an administrative centre for the National Trust but, during the Middle Ages, the legal and financial hub of the powerful Aberdaron and Bardsey *clas* community, equal in importance to the Clynnog Fawr community in the east. The court was traditionally known as the Court of the Lord of the Manor of Bardsey.

Directions

1 Make your way to the beach, turn right, climb the steps up to the headland and continue along the clear enough path as it heads due south. Descend the steps to the atmospheric Porth Meudwy (*porth*: harbour; *meudwy*: hermit) with its array of fishing boats, tractors, nets and lobster pots. This is where the pilgrims traditionally sailed to Bardsey and, indeed, where they still do, courtesy of a local boatman and his distinctive yellow catamaran. From Porth Meudwy climb the steps back up to the cliff path.

2 Continue along the fairly distinct paths. At the top of a set of well-maintained wooden steps ignore the new metal kissing-gate and continue to head south, alongside the fence. After the third wooden kissing-gate take the upper path alongside the stone wall. Just before the fence sweeps up the hill to the right, go through the kissing-gate and straight ahead to the rocky outcrop, just beyond which Bardsey hoves suddenly and dramatically into view. This is Pen y Cil, with its sheer drop into the agitated waters of Bardsey Sound.

3 From here climb up the reasonably clear, grassy path between the rocks and the fence. Make your way to the trig point and the National Trust plaque commemorating its purchase of the Pen y Cil headland in 1970. Head down the green lane. Go through the metal field gate and turn left towards the next field gate and waymark. Head west up the

field, Bardsey revealing some of its secrets now as the flatlands beyond the blank wall of cliff begin to come into view. Make for the kissing-gate at the top right hand corner of the field. Here, there is another NT plaque, announcing that this stretch of the headland is Bychestyn. Turn sharp left here.

4   Walk along the narrow green path towards the sheer drops at Parwyd. Follow the arrow pointing to the right and walk down through the gorse towards Bardsey and the sea. At the next little marker bear right. Stay on the lower of the more or less obvious paths towards Mynydd Gwyddel and Mynydd Mawr. As you continue closer and closer to the sea, turn right onto the little thin path towards the fence enclosing the old *clawdd* bank. Climb over the stile here and continue on up the lovely grassy path, following it round the big mound of gorse and rock. Head towards the rounded shape of Mynydd Gwyddel through two more stiles. Climb the reasonably clear path to the summit of Mynydd Gwyddel. There are wonderful, panoramic views from here. The low white building on the much higher Mynydd Mawr is the coastguard station. There was a large RAF presence here during the Second World War in anticipation of the invasion from the west that never materialised. Also, from the summit of Mynydd Gwyddel, the outline of the vanished Capel Mair, the pilgrim church of St Mary, is clearly visible in the grass slopes of Braich y Pwll, below. Head down the wide green path leading north from the summit.

5   If you wish to visit Ffynnon Fair, St Mary's Well, turn left at the green crossroads and follow the instructions below. To return to Aberdaron, turn right at the green crossroads, going around the end of the stone wall and continuing along the path before turning right onto the metalled road. Continue for about three quarters of a mile then turn right at Penbryn Bach and the now closed seafood restaurant. Go down the lane alongside the farm, through the field gate,

then through the kissing-gate in the far left hand corner of the field. More or less directly to your right across this next field you cross another stile and head for the little rusty kissing-gate. Go through the gate and down the couple of steps onto the lane. At the road turn right and, almost immediately left at the footpath sign up the steps and onto a path running the length of the *clawdd* bank. At the end of the path turn left onto the lane.

6   Continue along the lane, ignoring the footpath sign to Porth Meudwy (although you can, if you wish, return to Aberdaron by rejoining the cliff path at Porth Meudwy). You will eventually pass the gracious Cwrt, no longer the administrative base of the medieval church but of the National Trust in the area. It is also the operational centre for one of the Trust's social enterprise projects to safeguard and encourage the local fishing industry. From the road you will see a small blue boat in one of the farmhouse outbuildings. I understand this boat was donated by a very elderly local man whose father had built it and spent his working life in it, fishing and ferrying passengers across to Bardsey Island. The construction is, apparently, unique to the Aberdaron area, and is designed to withstand the specific stresses of the currents in the Sound.

7   At the crossroads turn right then almost immediately right again at the footpath sign. This is the site of the holy well, Ffynnon Sant, but it is badly neglected and barely visible beneath the invading brambles and bracken. Continue along the footpath until emerging onto the tarmac road. Descend this road into the village, to St Hywyn's Church, and back to the car-park.

Fynnon Fair
To visit St Mary's Well, go left at Point 5 above, and follow the valley down to where the little stream empties into the sea. There are medieval steps cut into the rock itself. It is not easy to

East wall

West wall and Norman door

spot the well, and impossible at high tide when it disappears beneath the water.

The Church
SH 173264
Access: The church is open throughout the year during daylight hours.

Around the middle of the sixth century Dyfrig, the Archbishop of Caerleon, together with a group of companions, including Cadfan, Hywyn, Maelrhys and Baglan, made their way to Llŷn and on to Bardsey, where Cadfan is credited with founding the Abbey. Maelrhys is associated with the little church above Porth Ysgo. Hywyn, probably the confessor to the early community on Bardsey, together with his brother Lleuddad, built his church here in Aberdaron, on the very margin of the Irish Sea and at the confluence of the rivers Seiont and Daron, which now flow beneath the bridges at the centre of the village.

St Hywyn's, like all the churches in Llŷn, was built and added to over several hundred years, the perfect Norman arch at the entrance possibly its oldest feature. Although not its oldest artefact. The inscribed late fifth-century memorial stones to 'Veracius' and 'Senacus', on display inside the church, testify to the likely presence of a very early Christian settlement at nearby Mynydd Analog.

But it is the location that most strongly evokes the ancient origins of this place: that steeply sloping churchyard teetering on the edge of the sea, and the simple church where the priest's words, as R. S. Thomas put it in another context, are 'drowned by the wind's caterwauling'. In his *A Description of Caernarvonshire*, the Regency era administrator Edmund Hyde Hall makes the somewhat bleak declaration that 'the parish must be regarded as irretrievably abandoned to the dominion of the blast'.

Bibliography

John Leland and Lucy Toulmin Smith, *The Itinerary of John Leland in Wales in or about the Years 1536–1539*, Pranava Books, 2009

Samuel Lewis, *A Topographical Dictionary of Wales*, S. Lewis & Co, 1849

Baring-Gould and Fisher, *The Lives of the British Saints*, Charles J. Clark, 1907

Edmund Hyde Hall, *A Description of Caernarvonshire 1809–1811*, Gwenlyn Evans, 1952

Gildas, *The Ruin and Conquest of Britain*, Hugh Williams (ed.), David Nutt, 1899

T. J. Hughes, *Wales's Best One Hundred Churches*, Seren, 2006

R. S. Thomas, *Collected Poems 1945–1990*, Phoenix, 1996

Byron Rogers, *The Man Who Went Into The West*, Aurum, 2006

Andrew Jones, *Every Pilgrim's Guide to Celtic Britain and Ireland*, Canterbury, 2002

R. Gerallt Jones, *A Place in the Mind*, Gomer, 2004

Adrian Bristow, *Dr Johnson & Mrs Thrale's Tour in North Wales 1774*, Bridge Books, 1995

Enid Roberts, *Bardsey Bound*, Y Lolfa, 2008

Christine Evans and Wolf Marloh, *Bardsey*, Gomer Press, 2008

Harri Webb, Enlli, in Dewi Roberts (ed.), *A Llŷn Anthology*, Gwasg Carreg Gwalch, 2008

Buglife, www.buglife.org.uk

James Dyer, *Hillforts of England and Wales*, Shire Publications, 1992

Directory of Open Churches, Bangor Diocese

Julian Heath, *Ancient Echoes: the early history of a Welsh peninsula*, Gwasg Carreg Gwalch, 2006

Barry Morgan, *Strangely Orthodox: R. S. Thomas and his Poetry of Faith*, Gomer, 2006

Richard Taylor, *How to Read a Church*, Rider, 2003

A. M. Allchin, *Praise Above All: Discovering the Welsh Tradition*, University of Wales, 1991

Clive Fewins, *The Church Explorer's Handbook*, Canterbury, 2005

Tim Prevett, *Roads and Trackways of North Wales*, Landmark, 2008

Donald Gregory, *Country Churchyards in Wales*,
Gwasg Carreg Gwalch, 2002

Terry John and Mona Rees, *Pilgrimage: a Welsh Perspective*,
Gomer, 2002

Pat O'Reilly and Sue Parker, *Wonderful Wildflowers of Wales*
Volumes 1–3, First Nature, 2005–07

Gwyn Williams, *Welsh Poets, Sixth Century to 1600*, Faber and
Faber, 1973

More Books
about Llŷn

Visit our website for further information:
www.carreg-gwalch.com

Orders can be placed on our
On-line Shop